RETURN
ENGAGEMENT

FACES
TO
REMEMBER–
THEN

NOW

Alexis Smith

RETURN ENGAGEMENT
FACES TO REMEMBER-THEN & NOW

BY JAMES WATTERS

WITH NEW PHOTOGRAPHS
BY HORST

Clarkson N. Potter, Inc./Publishers

DISTRIBUTED BY CROWN PUBLISHERS, INC. NEW YORK

For my parents

Many people contributed generously to this book. I must single out Ralph Graves, my former managing editor at the weekly *Life,* who with a swift vote of confidence picked up his telephone and made this project come together. I have always valued his advice and support, and never more than in making this book a reality.

I am indebted to John Springer and Don Smith in New York City, Marvin Page in Los Angeles and Jack Gage in Santa Barbara, who kindly introduced us to many of the actresses. Horst had two invaluable assistants, Johann Mayr, his longtime colleague, and Richard Stanley, who on the West Coast kept everything on the move. Designer Bob Ciano worked with his talented, reliable team of Ellen Kostroff, Sibbie Chalawick and Lou Valentino.

Others contributed more than they realized, and I am most grateful to Nikki Amdur, Betsy Bloomingdale, DeWitt Bodeen, Ronald Bowers, Ben Carbonetto, Susan Chadwick, David Chierichetti, Penny Costigan, the late George Cukor, Eleanor Debus, Gael Towey Dillon, Shirley Eder, Thomas Fulbright, Michael Fragnito, James Frasher, Milton Goldman, Bob Harman, Jane Hopper, Lloyd Ibert, Robert Kennedy, Marina Lakner, Yamilee Martelly, Gordon Mathews, Michael Maslansky, Joel McCrea, Dion McGregor, George C. Pratt, Melvin L. Scott, Donald Sewell, Richard J. Tardiff, Catherine Verret, Douglas Whitney and Roger Williams.

For picture research I owe thanks to Mary Corliss and Terry Geesken of the Museum of Modern Art/Film Stills Archive; Carlos Clarens and Howard Mandelbaum of Phototeque; and Marthe Smith and Gretchen Wessels of the Life Picture Service.

My very special thanks go to Lynn Nesbit, my agent; Paula Glatzer, without whom I could not have produced this book; and Carol Southern, the most bounteous and gentle of editors.

Designed by Bob Ciano

Vintage photo credits/Museum of Modern Art/Film Stills Archive: 12, 16, 19, 22, 40, 41, 47, 49, 52, 53, 70 right, 74, 78, 79, 91 (five), 95, 102, 104, 108, 126 top, 134, 141, 142, 144, 150 (two), 154, 164 bottom. Life Picture Service: 44, 133. Phototeque: 20. Douglas Whitney: 39, 58, 84, 92. Author's collection: 8-9, 10, 15, 25, 26, 28, 29, 30 (six), 32, 34 (two), 35 (two), 36 right (left-Horst), 43, 50, 55, 56, 62, 63, 64, 67 (two), 68 (two), 69 (two), 70 left (two), 73, 77, 81, 82, 88, 89, 96, 100, 101, 107 (four), 110, 112, 114-115, 116, 118, 120, 122, 126 bottom, 129 (two), 130, 131, 135, 137, 138, 147, 148, 149, 152, 153, 157, 159, 160, 161, 162, 164 top.

p. 132 "To Keep My Love Alive" Copyright © 1944 Harms, Inc. Warner Bros. Music

Published by Clarkson N. Potter, Inc., One Park Avenue, New York, New York 10016 and simultaneously in Canada by General Publishing Company Limited

Manufactured in the United States of America

Typographer: Publishers Phototype International Inc.
Printer: Rapoport

Library of Congress Cataloging in Publication Data

Watters, James.
Return Engagement.

Includes index.
1. Moving-picture actors and actresses—United States—Biography. 2. Actresses—United States—Biography. I. Horst, 1906-   . II. Title. PN1998.A2W35   1984   791.43'028'0922 [B]
84-16595 ISBN 0-517-55523-9

10 9 8 7 6 5 4 3 2 1
First Edition

CONTENTS

INTRODUCTION

Isabel Jewell was calling from a pay phone. Though she had appeared in 50 movies as a top-billed supporting player during a 40-year career, as well as in dozens of stage roles, she couldn't afford her own phone. Isabel said she would come for dinner if I met her cab—she didn't have six dollars for the fare. That evening at the Beverly Wilshire Hotel in Los Angeles, she poured out five hours of heartbreak on the triumphs and tragedies of being an actress. Broke and ill, she nonetheless had no regrets. Almost her last words were, "But you know, I still photograph. I can still look good."

That visit 14 years ago has stayed with me, as shall the 74 visits that make up this book. From the first encounter in 1979, when Horst, his assistant Hans Mayr and I showed up at Louise Brooks's hideaway in Rochester, New York, to begin an essay on nine memorable stars for *Life* magazine, through the completion of this book in March 1984, with the photographing of vivacious Ginger Rogers in Rancho Mirage, California, it has been an adventure of a lifetime for all of us. After the success of the *Life* article, it seemed only natural to go on, to photograph more actresses who have illumined our lives, affected our styles, haunted our dreams—then and now.

Life picture editor Mel Scott had recommended that Horst take on the original magazine assignment, and it was this suggestion that proved the key to everything. Here was a photographer, a contemporary of most of the subjects, whose style was both telling and timeless. With his masterful lighting, the ideal compliment for women of a certain age, Horst was able to capture the human side while not downplaying the aura of stardom—and without retouching, without soft lenses. His own personal touch, continental and gentlemanly of the old school, charmed all the women. Their smiles are real.

The selection is eclectic and entirely mine, made up of favorites from years of being a starstruck kid at the movies in Wyoming and attending the theater in New York and London. But frustration and sadness soon became part of the challenge of gathering these photographs and interviews. Irene Dunne, a breezy cutup in our numerous phone talks, said "no," that she wished to be remembered as she was in the movies. So did Deanna Durbin, who wrote from France that "after so many years of happy oblivion," she was pleased to be thought of. She sent along a snapshot of a trim and obviously content ex-star, just to set the rumors straight: "I can still pass under the Arc de Triomphe without holding my breath." Madeleine Carroll, living in southern Spain, spoke of her relief at being out of the limelight. She, too, enclosed a photo with her regrets, showing an absolutely stunning woman pushing 80.

These disappointments could be lived with. Others approached tragedy. Marlene Dietrich, one of her grandsons told me, would never face the public again, probably never emerge from her Paris apartment again. Rita Hayworth was already too ill with Alzheimer's disease when I reached her representatives. Madge Evans, Margaret Lindsay, Gloria Grahame and Mae West all said yes but in a matter of weeks were gone. Very fast, Horst and I became aware of time as never before, and it made our mission take on what we hadn't faced at the outset. This would be a historic documentation and, in too many cases, the last sitting. One actress in particular broke our hearts. I made three appointments with Dolores Del Rio. She canceled twice because of illness, and death canceled the third. Of all the ageless beauties, she was the most kindly, the most serene.

Looking back now, I have come to realize that never again will there be such a flowering of gifted, beautiful actresses. Before 1900 you could count the famous actresses of history (famous women of history, too, for that matter). As this century starts to come to a close, the great female stars are in short supply, especially when compared to the pre-1950s, when a magnificently large, healthy, productive, glamorous, trend-setting galaxy lighted up the arts. Whether they are etched in a single theatrical memory or captured on celluloid for all time, they had star power, staying power undimmed by age and the face of fashion. That's why the women who sat for Horst continue to fascinate with their not-so-fleeting charms, their rich, varied talents, their place as cultural phenomena.

That cranky old critic Percy Hammond once warned, "Never praise an actress because *it* will bite you." Here are 74 to prove him wrong. This homage sides with Jean Cocteau who believed, "Legends are lives that become history." Echoing Isabel Jewell, these actresses still look good—in every sense of the word.

James Watters
June 1984

Of the many assignments that have come my way during more than 50 years as a photographer, taking the portraits for this book was perhaps the most moving experience. I found myself invariably being received by my sitters with unforgettable smiles and touching kindness. Whether they were flourishing or ill, in hotels or hospitals, in rich houses or tiny apartments, they established an immediate personal contact.

Naturally I regret that some stars—Garbo, Dietrich, Bergman—could not be in this collection, since I had photographed them in the past and they have been my friends. But one can't have everything. Taking the photographs was a pleasure as well as a challenge. Every single star was unmistakably a professional and fully aware of what the camera can, and cannot, do. It wasn't nostalgia that inspired me, but respect—respect for talent and achievement and sheer hard work.

Horst
June 1984

MARY ASTOR

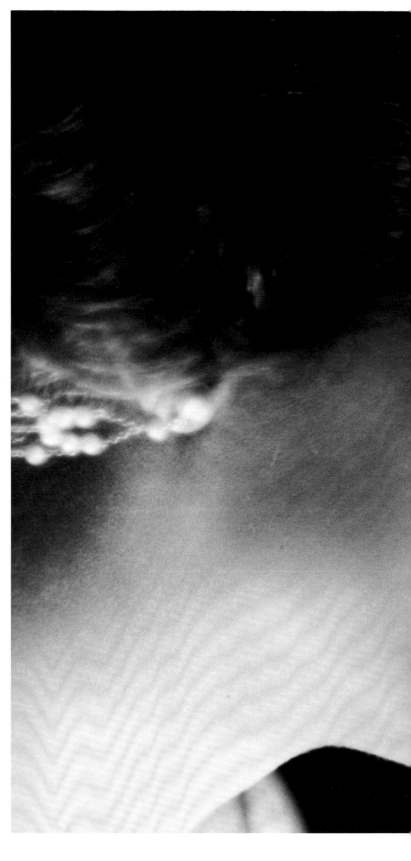

"**I**f you have to be institutionalized, then this is the best," says Mary Astor of the one-room cottage she shares with her canary, Prince Carol (of Rumania), at the Motion Picture Country House. "I've been here longer than any place I've ever lived before. But I am not charity, I pay my way." A heart attack and two strokes have left her in delicate health. Mary retired after making *Hush, Hush Sweet Charlotte* in 1965. But Mary's spirits are high. Seated cross-legged, she asks, "Mr. Horst, how many women my age, and after a stroke, can sit in a yoga position?" Concerned about her better side ("I broke my nose at 11 on roller skates"), she recalls working with Claudette Colbert. "The right side is my left side, if you get me, but Claudette was the star and her right side is like the other side of the moon; you never got a close-up." Mary still works hard. "My sixth novel has been sitting at a publisher's for years, probably too clean." Five others and two candid autobiographies detailing her affairs with John Barrymore and George S. Kaufman, bouts with booze, and redemption through Catholicism were praised and sold well. On the wall are her own sketches of her late Siamese and a caricature of the cast of *The Maltese Falcon*, the masterpiece with her most memorable role, the treacherous Brigid O'Shaughnessy. Here, too, is the Oscar for *The Great Lie*, the 1941 tearjerker she stole from Bette Davis. "Not $5 worth of gold in it, but I'm terribly grateful. I watch my old films," she says, "but it's like seeing ghosts, so many colleagues are gone." Then she smiles. "That's why I want my photo taken, so people won't think I'm dead yet." Mary makes one request. "If you run into Alan Alda, tell him he can put his shoes under my bed anytime." Her smile is the same she used at the end of *Dodsworth*, which to this day makes strong men weak in the knees.

BLANCHE SWEET

I've been through three natural disasters but they were rather fun. The San Francisco earthquake is still vivid with me. I remember the fires and the dynamiting of our building for backfire, and we all ended up going swimming at the Presidio. Then in 1930 I was in this terrific tornado, I guess you'd call it, in St. Paul, and later there was the Hurricane of '37, or was it '38, that hit Long Beach. But I'm telling you those three 'naturals' were nothing compared with the fourth I've lived through—what I call the Hollywood disaster." With the voice of a town crier, Blanche Sweet, all 4'11" of her, spits out the words, her tone ironic, her assessment candid.

By all rights, Blanche should be basking in the same sublime spotlight as her pioneer colleague and friend, the legendary Lillian Gish. "I was always more friendly with Dorothy (Lillian's late younger sister). She had a sense of humor. I was with her one really steamy summer night, leaving Lillian's apartment here in New York, when a masher came up and muttered a proposition or some obscenity. Dorothy looked him straight in the eye and said, 'Oh, please, it's too hot.' " The early lifestyles and careers of the Gishes paralleled hers to a point. Lillian and Blanche were born circa 1896; both had a traveling salesman as the father they never knew. "Well, I think I met my father once in Denver," recalls Blanche, "when he came backstage. He was a champagne salesman, quite a glamorous job, except he enjoyed it too much because he sampled his own product." Onstage from childhood, Lillian and Dorothy Gish were guided by their ambitious mother, Blanche by her dominating grandmother. Blanche and Lillian made their movie debuts within a year of each other for D. W. Griffith. Perhaps because Blanche was plumper and therefore looked older, she got a head start. She drew the title role in *The Lonedale Operator*, one of the most revolutionary of Griffith's melodramas. In that one, a fearless Blanche held off payroll bandits as Griffith advanced his cross-cutting editing techniques. Griffith then starred her in his first full-length feature, *Judith of Bethulia*, a landmark biblical epic that secures a place in film history for Blanche. "But I was stubborn, I was difficult, I played games, I was to fall in love, oh there are reasons and reasons," she confesses, to gloss over why she left the master filmmaker. By 1915 she was working with another name director, Cecil B. DeMille, who later said Blanche was the only star "I was ever afraid of." Ambitious, formidable, confident in her talent,

nothing fazed Blanche. "When I didn't know how to ride a horse," she says, "I wanted to do westerns." She finally met her match, dashing director Marshall Neilan, who besides being one of the finest (and still underrated) directors of the silent era, was also an infamous ladies' man. Mary Pickford, who could demand anyone to helm her movies, had Neilan direct her four times. After Blanche married "Mickey" in 1922, he refused to give up his favorite role, the great lover on the Hollywood scene. Gloria Swanson, Peggy Joyce Hopkins, Mary Miles Minter and Anna May Wong were among his conquests. By 1929 Blanche was ready for divorce and both were headed toward bankruptcy (she finally filed in 1933). Blanche's career had a few high points in the 1920s, mainly the first film version of *Anna Christie,* which after years of being lost was rediscovered in a Yugoslavian archive. It easily confirms Blanche's reputation as a great actress. Her *Tess of the D'Urbervilles* (in modern dress, no less) is on every international film archive's "most wanted" list for lost film classics. She made over 120 pictures altogether. Though she had a rich speaking voice and could sing, too, Blanche's career nose-dived after just three talkies. Determined to survive, she hit the Orpheum circuit. Touring, secondary Broadway roles, radio work

and a second marriage, to actor Raymond Hackett, brought stability if not financial reward in the '30s and '40s. Widowed in 1958, Blanche had to settle for clerking in a Los Angeles department store.

The serious film scholars started to seek her out in the late 1960s. She now lives in New York City in a one-room apartment with grandmother's picture front and center. "She was both mother and father to me." Blanche's reputation resuscitated, requests have poured in and Blanche has traveled to England and Italy and Canada to receive long overdue recognition as a pioneering movie actress. "Listen, I'm not like Lillian though. I don't know what I remember or if I remember what others have been telling me. They all think they know my work better than I do anyway." But Blanche does have a remarkable memory, and she always speaks her mind—telling off rude New York bus passengers or a waitress who brings her the wrong brand of beer. "I could never, never write a book. You have to be so *startling,*" she explains. "Well, I have a few 'startlings' rattling around in my closet, but they are personal and going to stay personal. After all, that has nothing to do with film or history or art. Let 'em look at my films to discover what I'm all about."

SYLVIA
SIDNEY

I have no curiosity about my past. For God's sake, I lived it." Sylvia Sidney is stretched out in the living room of her Connecticut clapboard, her prizewinning pugs locked in the kitchen making a terrible racket. "I just don't believe all that living in the past is healthy." She yells at the dogs. "That bitch of mine, nothing frightens her." For the actress many have called the greatest emotional star of her generation—"I got paid by the tear"—Sylvia sings no sad songs for herself. Born Sophia Kosow in New York in 1910, and taking the name of her dentist stepfather, she made her stage debut at 15. "Jed Harris (the producer) used to tell me to come back when the milk was dry behind my ears," she says. In 1931 she replaced Clara Bow in *City Streets* and became "the proletarian princess of Paramount," crying her way through unwed motherhood (*An American Tragedy, Confessions of a Co-ed*) or behind bars (*Ladies of the Big House, Mary Burns, Fugitive*). She has the distinction of being the only star for whom a prophylactic was named. "That was in Japan after I made that lousy film version of *Madame Butterfly* (with Cary Grant), so they called the things Sylvia Sidneys. I couldn't sue, but I should have asked for a cut."

Working for demanding directors like William Wyler and Fritz Lang, she took up needlepoint, for which she would become famous in the 1950s. But Lang gave her her greatest roles in *Fury* and *You Only Live Once*. Stage and television work, though considerable, never measured up to the films she made in the 1930s, but she has continued to be a working actress now for 60 years. Three marriages (publisher Bennett Cerf, actor Luther Adler, agent Carlton Alsop) failed, and recently she had fits over Budd Schulberg's memoirs, which painted her as the mistress of his father, B. P. Schulberg, who headed Paramount during her starring years. But Sylvia claims no secrets and willingly speaks out about the sadness in her life—her cataract problems and the amyotrophic lateral sclerosis that struck down her only son, Joey Adler. "When it was discovered my son had it, there was no place to go to find out about this dreaded (Lou Gehrig's) disease. These are the important things in life and not what it's like to have kissed Spencer Tracy or Gary Cooper."

DOROTHY LAMOUR

In the red-white-and-blue years of World War II, Dorothy Lamour was as popular as FDR. She was one of the top 10 stars at the box office and *Life* magazine published a poll listing her as "The No. 1 Pin-Up Girl of the U.S. Army." A blonde named Betty Grable, who became her dear friend, and a redhead named Rita Hayworth gave Dottie tough competition, but she was already a national treasure. She proved it best, not with her good-natured clowning with Edgar Bergen and Charlie McCarthy on radio or by playing straight woman to the antics of Bing Crosby and Bob Hope in the *Road* pictures, but by giving of herself tirelessly. At her own expense, she raised as much as $50 million in war bonds. In her North Hollywood bungalow, among autographs from Truman, Eisenhower, Nixon, Johnson and Reagan, hangs her pride and glory, the citation for being Uncle Sam's Super War Bond Salesgirl. And over the entrance to this unpretentious home is a horseshoe, a small one, given to her in 1931 on the eve of winning the Miss New Orleans beauty contest. "I've been lucky," Dorothy says. "God took me by the hand, and in return I have always tried to give my helping hand to others."

Born Mary Leta Dorothy Kaumeyer in a New Orleans charity ward in 1914, she knew poverty as a kid. With big dark eyes and a comely teenage figure, she was show biz bound. Her singing voice, deep and liquid, helped. A generation of young men would swoon hearing her coo "Moon of Manakoora" in John Ford's *The Hurricane* in 1937. From New York chanteuse, Dorothy was soon sashaying around Paramount in an Edith Head creation called the sarong. The Smithsonian has one in its collection. "My sarong may have been a shocker, but it looks like long underwear today. I'll tell you a secret, it's what I did with it that counts." She adds, "But don't get me wrong, I was never a fan of myself. I could never stand to watch myself on the screen. I always said the damned sarong kinda held me back. You see one South Sea epic, you've seen 'em all." In only a handful of her 50-odd movies did she play a jungle princess, but Paramount promoted that limited image or else kept her close to Crosby and Hope. Maybe that's why her popularity waned, and by the mid-1950s she was content to rear her two sons from a second marriage to William Howard of the Baltimore horsey set. The nadir came when Crosby and Hope heartlessly gave Joan Collins the lead in *Road to Hong Kong,* relegating Dorothy to a cameo. The Lamour lure suffered but was not snuffed out. She did television guest spots, stock, club dates, and while the critics weren't always kind, the fans showed up. When her husband of 35 years died in 1978, she emerged from a half year of depression with an upbeat autobiography, then took up the crusade to get widows off their "kaoholes"—Hawaiian for backsides.

In 1983, Dorothy became a grandmother and celebrated 50 years in show business. President Reagan and Nancy wired: "When they toast your wonderful career, count us in; when they mention your unparalleled contribution to this nation in World War II, we agree wholeheartedly; and when they applaud one of the brightest stars to ever shine in the Hollywood firmament, ours will be the loudest clapping you hear." Another friend used perfect 1940-ese: "Let's face it, Dottie's a livin' doll." At Paramount, her home from 1936 to 1952, they still offer a specialty in the commissary: fresh pineapple, sliced bananas, strawberries with cream cheese, a.k.a. the Dorothy Lamour salad.

The nondescript house is nestled in the Brentwood section of Los Angeles. It is not what a Hollywood home is imagined to be. Too many books—good books, classics, dusty but obviously read. The backyard is pool-less and overrun with cats—13 to be exact. The furniture is solid stuff from the '30s, and the two Oscars on view are as dusty as the books. An inscribed photograph reads: "To Evelyn and Hal—From the old matchmaker with affection. Will Rogers." Another reads: "To Evelyn—My dear little son of a bitch. If I didn't love Hal, I'd kill him. Respectfully yours, Jim Cruze." This well-lived-in place befits its mistress. Evelyn Venable never went Hollywood. She may have been a lust object for a vet director like Cruze, and she did snag a great cinematographer, Hal Mohr (the Oscars are his for *A Midsummer Night's Dream* and the Claude Rains *Phantom of the Opera*), but as the daughter and granddaughter of scholars, Evelyn didn't find happiness until she went back to college and ended up a teacher herself. "When I enrolled at UCLA, my daughter was a sophomore and I was a freshman. Then our younger daughter followed and everyone got confused," explains the imposing, handsome woman who hasn't made a movie since 1943. "I studied classical languages, got a Phi Beta Kappa and became a member of the faculty. My students never heard of Evelyn Venable."

Her films have not exactly disappeared. *David Harum* with Rogers, *Death Takes a Holiday* with Fredric March and *The Little Colonel* with Shirley Temple continue to play. And in *Alice Adams,* Evelyn, the haughty incarnation of the rich snob, gives Katharine Hepburn the air. "But I was wild about teaching in the sense I was never wild about acting," she says, "and I wasn't a dummy. That's why I married a cameraman. We were together 40 years (Mohr died in 1974). My roles got worse and I wanted to have a family, and they came first." A woman of conviction, Evelyn is a strict vegetarian and swears that she has never tasted "any organism that has a conscious life. I even feed my cats a vegetarian diet."

Born in Cincinnati in 1913, Evelyn first acted in school Shakespeare directed by her father, Emerson Venable, a Shakespearean teacher of some reputation. Through him she met Walter Hampden and traveled with his rep company, playing Ophelia to the aged actor's Hamlet. Paramount scouts took notice, and in 1933 she made her debut in *Cradle Song.* Her co-workers warmed to Evelyn more than moviegoers, who found her a touch too Victorian in the Depression era of flashy, fleshy ingenues. Still, she looked right in hoopskirts and sunbonnets, and was mighty pretty sitting in a buggy or walking under a parasol by a bubbling brook. When Horst started to shoot, the scholar turned ingenue once again. Like a pro, Evelyn warned: "Watch the spot on my nose—I got it banging into a rabbit-hutch door as a child, and maybe you better cheat the eyes. Remember, I lived with a cameraman for years."

EVELYN VENABLE

GALE SONDERGAARD

By Los Angeles standards, Echo Park is a ghetto. The graffiti matches that of any depressed urban area on the East Coast and Spanish is heard as frequently as English. In a little frame house with a well-tended garden cut out of the cement backyard lives one of the martyrs of the blacklist. Gale Sondergaard, willowy, hard of hearing and as lined as Isak Dinesen, is a compelling figure of a woman in her 80s. Her awesome presence still packs a charge, just as it did between 1936 and 1947 when she was a classy movie meanie—the seductive Nazi agent in *My Favorite Blonde*, Tylette the cat in *The Blue Bird*, the sor-

ceress in *A Night in Paradise*, and of course all those sinister housekeepers in *The Cat and the Canary, The Black Cat, The Climax* and *Anthony Adverse* (her film debut, for which Gale won the best supporting actress Oscar the first year that award was presented in 1936). Proud and dignified, Gale has been less like her most famous roles—the Spider Woman in the Sherlock Holmes series and the Eurasian wife who murders Bette Davis in *The Letter*—than those parts calling for rectitude, respect and wisdom—the wife of Dreyfus in *The Life of Emile Zola* and Lady Thiang, the number one wife, in *Anna and the King of Siam*, her second Oscar nomination.

Today Gale sheds no tears. Though she didn't work in films between 1949 and 1969, she says matter-of-factly, "I personally have put the blacklist behind me." Her Hollywood career was squashed by the witch-hunts of the House Un-American Affairs Committee investigating the "infiltration of subversive propaganda into motion pictures." Her husband, Herbert Biberman, the writer-director and a founder of the Directors Guild, went to prison as one of the Hollywood Ten, that group who chose to challenge HUAC, refused to name names and were cited for contempt. Subpoenaed herself in 1951, she took the Fifth Amendment when asked if she was or had ever been a member of the Communist Party. Five years later, called to testify again, Gale was an articulate defender of her political rights. She remained unemployed for 20 years, except for a one-woman show of play excerpts she fashioned for herself. Her first real break came when she returned to her native Minnesota to appear in rep at the Tyrone Guthrie Theatre in Minneapolis in 1967. Her alma mater, the University of Minnesota, gave her an "outstanding achievement award" for her acting in 1968, and a year later she made the Hollywood breakthrough in a stage production of *The Crucible*, Arthur Miller's play about the Salem witch-hunts, and in a guest appearance on the television series *It Takes a Thief*. Her husband didn't live to see Gale's comeback in the 1970s. Her last role, as a medium, was in 1982 in a cheapie called *Echoes*. While she has come to terms without bitterness, there is a sense of loss, she admits, the loss of work that might have been. It's a loss we all share.

ANNABELLA

No, no, I don't put my leg on the chair. No, that would start rumors again I am a lesbian. Just let me give you a big, big smile." Annabella's smile helped to launch her as the first great French star of the sound era. Thanks to the genius of René Clair, her gamin charms were given full range in his classic celebrations of the *vie de bohème*, *Le Million* and *Quatorze Juillet.* Annabella is also remembered as the dominating older woman who stole Tyrone Power's heart when he was Hollywood's pretty boy matinee idol and in doing so brought down the ire of their 20th Century-Fox boss, Darryl F. Zanuck. A 1939 marriage more or less ended when Power joined the Marines in 1942, and they finally divorced in 1948. But, says Annabella, "we were always friendly to the end." Power took two more wives, as well as several mistresses, and died in 1958 at age 45. Recent biographies have called him "bisexual." The rumors about her own sexual preference date from 1946, she thinks, when she starred on Broadway in Jean-Paul Sartre's *No Exit.* "As the homosexual, Annabella is giving a bold and calculated performance that packs one corner of Hell with horror," wrote Brooks Atkinson in *The New York Times.* Annabella never remarried and continues to use Power's name—"To me it means memories of fun and much happiness." Today she lives in Paris and also on a farm near Biarritz, devoting her time to prison reform. "I work with young people to try to aid them in a difficult world." She comes to the States often to see her daughter (the ex-Mrs. Oskar Werner) from an earlier marriage to actor Jean Murat. Her conversation, though, is peppered with Power. "Yes, he did have one fault, but only one—he could never say 'no' to anyone." She points to a heart-shaped pin of diamonds and rubies she is wearing. "Ty gave it to me when he left for war and told me, 'I'll always be close to your heart.' He still is."

INA CLAIRE

In 1907 Ina Claire made her stage debut on the Orpheum vaudeville circuit, imitating Sir Harry Lauder, the Scottish comedian. In 1915 she introduced "Hello, Frisco, Hello" in the Ziegfeld Follies to celebrate the opening of the first transcontinental telephone line between New York and San Francisco. By 1929 she had taken John Gilbert away from Garbo and made the cover of *Time*. When she retired in 1954 to become one of the grande dames of San Francisco society, marrying her third husband, wealthy lawyer William Wallace, Jr., Ina was acclaimed the most brilliant American stage comedienne ever. She still has no rivals, and unlike other notable stage stars, Lynn Fontanne, Katharine Cornell and Laurette Taylor, Ina has left a legacy on film to cement forever her exalted reputation. If she had been born after the turn of the century rather than in 1892, she would have been a more important movie star. By 1930s standards she was over the hill and could not compete with the younger actresses who came from the stage—Claudette Colbert, Irene Dunne, Ann Harding. But Ina's importance in the theater is historic. Because "her command of the spoken word was matchless," as one critic put it, "she could cover the whole range of a play's speech in much the same way a great coloratura singer expresses all the notes of an aria." More than any other performer, Ina freed the modern stage of the artificial, declamatory style of the Edwardian period by using natural, almost chatty speech. It was said, too, that her own dialogue was often wittier than what she got from her writers, from S. N. Behrman to T. S. Eliot (her farewell was in Eliot's *The Confidential Clerk*). Today, living at the top of Nob Hill and surrounded by mementos of a memorable life—Cecil Beaton sketches of her on the bedroom wall and love letters from F. Scott Fitzgerald stuck in a bureau drawer—Ina is a vivacious nonagenarian who can still outtalk all her visitors. Her friend Roger Williams looks after her and they make a comic duo. Reclining on her white-on-white Syrie Maugham sofa, the elegant Ina carries on about the latest social scandal or how the oriental cook, upset over some minor slight, has thrown the evening's dinner on the floor. She steadfastly refuses to reminisce—"The memory does *not* linger on." Like the Duchess of Windsor, Ina can be vague. Looking down on the city below, she speaks of Paris and Rome and Salzburg. Roger reassures her that they have not left the city by the bay. "Oh, hell," Ina protests, "why do I have to be exact at my age?" It is impossible to believe her champagne laughter has nearly spanned the century.

LOUISE BROOKS

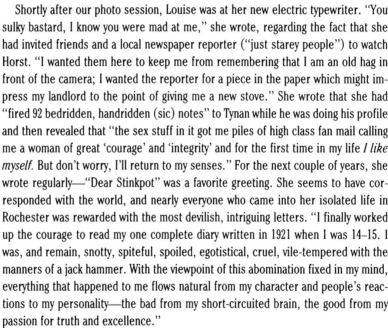

It has been nearly three decades since Louise Brooks, a forgotten face from the pre-Depression era, was rediscovered by the French critics. Since then an industry has grown up in praise of this extraordinary cult figure. Revivals of her silent American movies and particularly *Diary of a Lost Girl* and *Pandora's Box,* the masterpieces she made in Germany for director G. W. Pabst, have affirmed her transcendent abilities. Louise, in the words of the great film historian Lotte Eisner, "needed no directing, but could move across the screen causing the work of art to be born by her mere presence." Kenneth Tynan's 1979 *New Yorker* profile, using chunks of Louise's own writing and words, introduced her to a wider audience by spilling the lowdown on her alcoholism (she was "gin-coherent" until 1974), promiscuity (at one point she had affairs going with three rich men who never realized the truth), fondness for Proust (she can quote whole passages) and a wicked, wicked tongue (she once told me, "How I'd adore meeting Ina Claire, and how we could chop up all the bastards we knew"). In 1982, Louise published *Lulu in Hollywood,* a collection of articles she had written for "little" cinema magazines over the years. It was a smash. Her memory is pitiless, if a bit faulty, and she's a first-rate stylist. From her tiny apartment in Rochester, New York, where she moved in the 1950s at the instigation of James Card, then film curator of George Eastman House, Louise recalls the glories and occasional squalor of her past in prose both clear and cutting. Arthritic and frail ("82 pounds this week"), she conquers new worlds with her seductive, often poisonous letters.

Shortly after our photo session, Louise was at her new electric typewriter. "You sulky bastard, I know you were mad at me," she wrote, regarding the fact that she had invited friends and a local newspaper reporter ("just starey people") to watch Horst. "I wanted them here to keep me from remembering that I am an old hag in front of the camera; I wanted the reporter for a piece in the paper which might impress my landlord to the point of giving me a new stove." She wrote that she had "fired 92 bedridden, handridden (sic) notes" to Tynan while he was doing his profile and then revealed that "the sex stuff in it got me piles of high class fan mail calling me a woman of great 'courage' and 'integrity' and for the first time in my life *I like myself.* But don't worry, I'll return to my senses." For the next couple of years, she wrote regularly—"Dear Stinkpot" was a favorite greeting. She seems to have corresponded with the world, and nearly everyone who came into her isolated life in Rochester was rewarded with the most devilish, intriguing letters. "I finally worked up the courage to read my one complete diary written in 1921 when I was 14–15. I was, and remain, snotty, spiteful, spoiled, egotistical, cruel, vile-tempered with the manners of a jack hammer. With the viewpoint of this abomination fixed in my mind, everything that happened to me flows natural from my character and people's reactions to my personality—the bad from my short-circuited brain, the good from my passion for truth and excellence."

Louise grew up in Cherryvale and Wichita, Kansas, the second of four children of an intellectual lawyer. Her mother was artistic and let the children go their willful ways. Louise was kicked out of the Wichita College of Music at 15 for being "insulting," and her parents then let the teenager travel to New York City to study dance with Ted Shawn. But she was thrown out of Denishawn Dancers, too, and a certain pattern set in, which years later would cause her to consider "Escaping with My Life" as the title for *Lulu in Hollywood.* Her Paramount films in the mid-1920s brought her a brief vogue, and the Dixie Dugan comic strip paid homage to Louise's

patent-leather bangs. In 1929, she refused to dub the sound version of *The Canary Murder Case,* and in doing so, ruined her reputation in Hollywood. On the way down, she was part of a dance team at the Plaza Hotel, did some radio and ended up working as a clerk at Saks Fifth Avenue until she was saved by an internationally famous tycoon who supports her with an allowance to this day. Her marriage to director Edward Sutherland was brief, and her affair with George Marshall, the millionaire who owned the Washington Redskins and made a fortune in the laundry business—she called him "Wet Wash"—was disastrous. She confessed, "How can I explain George being the rock upon which my self-esteem was shattered? His direct, plainspoken cruelty was felt and known to all. From our first meeting I knew he was dangerously destructive. It wasn't love or sex or respect or a need to be told what to do— my mother turned me loose at birth and autonomous I have remained—what kept me enthralled?" Louise returned to him again and again until his death.

Nowadays Louise's letters have dwindled to brief, hand-written notes on colored slips of paper. She plans no more memoirs, though she admits, "my memories flow so easily, it scares me. I follow the rule of my beloved Proust. 'The duty of the writer is not to imagine, but to perceive reality.' My memory is selective, but what I remember is as clear as if it were recorded on film." From her bedridden state, Louise has made her own special world, and in it she is quite capable of twisting everything into a dramatic situation and then getting an emotional exercise out of it. But Louise knows better than any of her idolaters that she is unique and ranks with Garbo and Gish as one of the goddesses supreme of the cinema.

ELEANOR POWELL

In the fall of 1935, when Mussolini was eyeing Ethiopia and Hitler was reclaiming the Saar, a 23-year-old hoofer from Springfield, Massachusetts, was conquering Broadway. Eleanor Powell was literally working both sides of the street. At the Winter Garden she was hailed as "the world's greatest feminine tap dancer" in the Dietz-Schwartz revue *At Home Abroad,* holding her own with Beatrice Lillie and Ethel Waters. Directly across Broadway at Loew's Capitol, Eleanor was kicking high and tapping madly in her second film, *Broadway Melody of 1936,* stealing the spot from Jack Benny. For the next eight years, Eleanor had no peer. Her feats of tap and dance extravaganza were unbelievably challenging. In *Rosalie,* using Cole Porter's title song, she darted from one oversized drum to the next, leaping through hoops of fire, to tap out chorus after chorus against a backdrop of 2,000 prancing extras. A female Fred Astaire, she did her own choreography, working out every step like an engineer. It was a strange process. She would conceive the routine, do the number in ballet slippers for the orchestra to lay down the track in a recording studio, then film the dance silently. "The camera and crew made too much noise to do it any other way," she explains. Then it was back to the recording room to synchronize the taps with the edited film. "Do you know how hard it was to redo those fancy, intricate little tap steps?" she asks 40 years later, only to recall in detail every single movement she ever committed to film. Her shining hour came with Astaire, dancing "Begin the Beguine" in *Broadway Melody of 1940.* This exhilarating sequence, with long master takes, could only have been accomplished by two matchless perfectionists. In 1943 Eleanor married dimpled dandy Glenn Ford and ended her career as his took off. It was a mistake made for love. Eleanor thought she should devote herself to her husband and their son, Peter. In the 1950s she won five Emmys for her *Faith of Our Children* television series, but she never considered this religious work a form of show business. By 1959 she had had enough of a bad marriage. She divorced Ford, and at the urging of her son, made a triumphant comeback on the nightclub circuit. But by the late 1960s she again had faded from view. With the release of the compilation musical *That's Entertainment,* a new generation discovered the hypnotic powers of Powell. She was slow coming to grips with the adoration, though her fans, the most loyal of any star after those of Jeanette MacDonald, had always remained steadfast. Eleanor was grateful, signing stills, "Whenever you hear the beat of my feet, it is really the beat of my heart saying thank you and God bless you." Sadly, the Powell renaissance, filled with revivals and tributes, had not yet peaked when she died of cancer in 1982. Frank Sinatra said, "The likes of her we'll never see again." Years earlier another Italian, Arturo Toscanini, confessed: "Three things I will carry through life—the glorious sunset, the splendor of the Grand Canyon and the dancing of Eleanor Powell."

COLLEEN MOORE

"**M**y old movie eyes (one blue, one brown) have seen just about everything." Colleen Moore knows whereof she speaks. If any star can tell you where the bodies are buried, it's this eternal flapper. To a generation she may have represented the jazz age with all its gay accent on youth and its nose-thumbing at the leftovers from the Edwardian era, but Colleen was one jazz baby who always had her head screwed on straight. Looking back on her imitators from Clara Bow to Joan Crawford, she surely has had the last laugh. "I was mighty lucky, and very glad I was never a beauty. The beauties suffered the most." After a long apprenticeship, Colleen emerged in 1923 as a major star, rivaling Mary Pickford in popularity with her 35th movie, *Flaming Youth.* Like Mary, she had a keen business mind. Today, with her helmet of black bangs and short bob reminiscent of the flapper days, Colleen is one of the richest women in America and, of course, a Republican. She's Patti Davis Reagan's godmother, and her dearest friend is Clare Boothe Luce, with whom she globe-trots at a ring of the phone. "When Clare calls and says, 'Let's go shopping,' she usually means for me to hop a plane and do Hong Kong," Colleen explains. "On our last trip Clare wanted to drop in on Indira Gandhi, and I think if she had brought the right dress, we might have gone all the way to Rome to say hello to the Pope." Colleen lives on a ranch in Templeton, California, and among its treasures is a Thai temple

she picked up on one of her recent trips to the East. "At the moment I'm dealing with my new Chinese help too. I teach them three words of English a day."

Colleen was born in Port Huron, Michigan, in 1902, and her father, a successful engineer, moved the family from Tampa to Atlanta to Detroit. Colleen says she was "stagestruck from my earliest memory." Her uncle, Walter Howey, editor of the Chicago *American,* was the prototype for the unscrupulous managing editor in the Hecht-MacArthur play *The Front Page.* Howey helped D. W. Griffith fight the Chicago censor board when it tried to cut the orgy scenes from *Intolerance,* and as a favor Griffith got the 14-year-old Colleen a screen test. A natural comedienne who developed into a fine dramatic actress, she wrote about her experiences in *Silent Star,* a bestseller in 1969, but too many of her peers were still alive then for her to unearth all the skeletons. "I don't want to hurt people and I'll never do an update. I don't mind telling you that Spencer (Tracy) would disappear for four or five days with his drinking problems (she made her best talkie, *The Power and the Glory,* with him) or that Orson Welles shouldn't take all the credit for *Citizen Kane* when it was Herman Mankiewicz (the screenwriter) who was really letting go on Hearst. But why should I, at this point, say who really fathered Gloria Swanson's 'adopted' son?" Colleen is chuckling gently. "Even at my age, I believe in looking forward more than looking back." In December 1983, she had enough faith in the future to take her fourth husband and go traipsing off to Switzerland for a Christmas honeymoon.

BETTE DAVIS

If I lived in a tent in the Sahara, you'd know I was from New England." Surrounded by her Toby mugs and " good old Yankee furniture," Bette Davis strikes a kitchen match for the ever-present cigarette on the underside of a heavy field table. "I couldn't sell my furniture if I wanted to, the way I've treated my favorite things. There are match marks under everything," she barks in her best *Baby Jane* voice, patting the table as if to soothe the savage blow. Scattered here and there are needlepoint pillows, trumpeting the catchwords of a career. "What a Dump!" "No Guts, No Glory." "Old Age Ain't No Place for Sissies." Bette may have been born in Lowell, Massachusetts (in 1908) and retreated to Maine and Connecticut during the low times of an up-and-down career in the 1950s and '60s, but in the 1970s she came back to Hollywood to make her final home. She says one day she'll rest in a Los Angeles cemetery

next to her best friend, perhaps the only real friend and companion she ever had, her mother, Ruthie. Bette's apartment building is smack in the middle of "boys' town," that section of West Hollywood dominated by the gays who are worshipful fans of Judy Garland, Mae West, Marilyn Monroe and, of course, Davis. From her terrace, Bette can look down on the Spanish stucco-style remnants of the

'20s and '30s, including an old apartment house with an inner courtyard that was her first residence when she arrived in 1931. "When I started in Hollywood, all was lies. The publicity machines just ground them out. Well, I was willing to work to impress, but not by lies. I had my pride." She lets out a howl. "Yes, I had pride, when what I needed was hips. I have no hips, never did, no fanny either. Karl Freund (the German cinematographer) told me I had great eyes. Well, I lasted at Universal for over a year on my eyes, though my legs weren't too

bad. Then they fired me, and when Universal fired you, nobody wanted you." A familiar litany is under way.

Bette has always been adept at reciting her own colorful, highly edited version of the rise and fall and rise again of Hollywood's undisputed dowager queen. She plays down how at her peak she settled for weak directors so she could call the shots herself. She is less than forthright about her failed marriages (four) and her lovers (from Milquetoastish actor George Brent to domineering director William Wyler to billionaire Howard Hughes—biographer Charles Higham claims Bette helped cure Hughes's impotence). And she has never spelled out the heartbreak of her family troubles.

Sister Barbara, a failed actress, was in and out of sanitariums until her death. The daughter Bette adopted when married to actor Gary Merrill, her last husband, is brain damaged and has been in a special home for over 30 years. Ruthie, of course, was a stage mother, but Bette gets terribly defensive on that point. "Well, she was *never* a wild stage mother like Ginger Rogers's or Greer Garson's." Nowadays Bette prefers to quote Ruthie when it comes to all the

skeletons in the closet. "My mother always said it's the best fruit the birds pick on!"

Fussing with Bette's fine, thin hair is Peggy Shannon, Joan Crawford's hairdresser until Bette hired her in the early 1970s to be a personal helpmate. The woman is angular and silent, a chain-smoker like her mistress, who is ram-

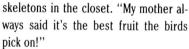

bling on about everything from what "a lousy actor little Ronald Reagan was in the Warner Bros. days" to the decline of the acting profession. "Nobody respects the tradition of training, and I tell you the joy in the work itself is gone. This new crowd only talks about how much money they earn. Disgusting," she hammers home. "Sometimes it's damned hard to go along with the world the way it is today. I loved my work and nothing would please me more than being remembered for being a good worker."

Horst interrupts to ask for a smile. "A smile? That's not my natural tendency. I am an unsmiling woman," she says, as a coquettish smirk crosses her thin lips. "You'd get a bigger smile if I thought I could go back to age 50. Women should stop physically at 40. Men? Maybe 50. Why, why do we have to get old?"

In the summer of 1983, this fierce, feisty fighter entered a New York hospital complaining of pains and nearly didn't come out. Following a mastectomy, Bette suffered a stroke. At 75, she had to drop out of a highly touted role in the television series *Hotel,* her great acting days at an end. Though in retrospect too many of her performances come across

as outlandish, old-fashioned and terribly sentimental, the Davis personality, with its unique brand of neuroticism, continues to give good value. You simply can't take your eyes off the sight. While Horst adjusted his key light, Bette held her pose patiently in a Yankee wingback chair. "My mother was a photographer, you know, and she was a great retoucher. I hope you are." Horst asked if the light was too bright or too hot. True to her style, Bette crowed, "I like 'em hot."

LUISE RAINER

There are two schools of thought about Luise Rainer. One paints her as the fragile flower from Vienna, shy, lonely, almost tragic, who became the victim of two men. Louis B. Mayer, the tyrannical boss who wanted her "to sit on my lap like my other stars do," vowed to destroy her if she left MGM. Clifford Odets, the self-destructive "genius" playwright who wed Luise at the peak of her brief career, broke her heart. The other side coldly classifies Luise as "froufrou and forged steel," "part *mittel-Europa* charmer, part con-artist." Face-to-face, Luise is a traffic cop. Swinging her arms, grasping her breastbone, eyes popping, she exclaims, "I've always had a chicken neck. When I came to America I gorged myself on apple pie and ice cream and I never had a weight problem. Today in Switzerland I live on cheese and chocolate." The first actress to win two successive Oscars, she swears, "I never really liked what I did and I was not happy; it was frightening. I didn't want to sell myself, I wanted to do beautiful things, to give, to feel, with my *guts*."

For 45 years Luise has been overdramatizing her tale of the innocent in Hollywood. Of her nine movies, a couple are campy (*The Great Waltz, Dramatic School*—she's the ace student among Lana Turner, Ann Rutherford and Paulette Goddard); another is quite romantic and spectacular (*The Great Ziegfeld*—her legendary telephone crying scene, which was almost cut from the finished film, is in retrospect not really Oscar caliber: "Hello, Flo? . . . Yes, this is Anna . . . It's all so wonderful and I'm so happy . . . I hope you are happy too"); and one holds up as old-fashioned narrative (*The Good Earth*—Mme. Chiang Kai-shek, after seeing Luise as the obedient wife, O-lan, reportedly thought she was really Chinese). The latter is a marvelously disciplined job, coming from an actress more mannered than modest. Visconti and Fellini, attracted to her florid style, tried to woo her with comeback roles.

Happily married since 1944 to now retired British publisher Robert Knittel, several years her junior, Luise did make a mini-comeback in the last few years. In New York, Los Angeles and Boston, she appeared in one-night stands of Tennyson's *Enoch Arden,* a 90-minute feat of memory if nothing else. Like other old stars, she succumbed to TV's *Love Boat.* To Joe Franklin, TV's nostalgia addict, she confessed, "I live in an old Roman village with cobblestones, well, actually pre-Roman, and I walk and walk (pause) I walk in beauty." Self-parody and sentimentality have joined her small repertoire. Considering her career ended in 1943 with a war drama, *Hostages,* Luise has coddled the mystique with finesse, resurfacing often enough to be newsy, yet not so often that she can't get away with the same dialogue. She has never been consistent about basic facts, particularly her birth date—1909 is generally accepted. It is far too late to speculate what might have happened if old man Mayer had given her better parts or if she hadn't gotten mixed up with a suicidal case like Odets. In *The Emperor's Candlesticks,* playing a countess, Luise grins ear to ear from beginning to end. At one point, the ever debonair William Powell is compelled to inquire of his co-star: "Has anyone ever told you you have a relentless smile?" Sometimes life does imitate the movies.

MARGARET
O'BRIEN

Except for a wretchedly unconvincing turn, flavored by a phony French accent, in the 1944 *Jane Eyre* with Joan Fontaine, Margaret O'Brien gave a series of psychologically acute performances that awed critics and enthralled movie fans during the World War II years. As the orphan in *Journey for Margaret*, the waif in *Lost Angel*, Judy Garland's baby sister in *Meet Me in St. Louis* (singing "Drunk Last Night"), this skinny, bite-size Circe was compared to prodigies like Mozart and Menuhin. Critic James Agee wrote that in *Meet Me in St. Louis* "glints of her achievement hypnotize me as thoroughly as anything since Garbo." When her cow Elizabeth, in *Our Vines Have Tender Grapes*, was trapped in the burning barn, a pigtailed Margaret flooded a nation with tears. Tales that she cried on cue if a director, or worse her mother, mentioned Margaret's dead dog do not discredit her amazing talent. Most child whizzes flunk the transitional teen years, and Margaret was no exception. Though she braved Broadway and live television, she was an ex-star by the 1960s. Now living with her second husband outside Los Angeles, she works occasionally (in the 1981 Disney movie, *Amy,* she had sixth billing) and she says she'd like to work more. The day of the photo session Margaret arrives at the Beverly Wilshire Hotel in Beverly Hills carrying a fancy ball gown and tiara. She jokes about being too old "to play dress up." But standing on the grand staircase, decked out in her make-believe finery, her enormous Irish-Spanish eyes aglow, the years fall away.

JANE WITHERS

In 1938 Jane Withers ranked eighth between Myrna Loy and Alice Faye in the top 10 at the box office. Today she remains a Hollywood fixture, doing charity work and guest starring on television. Her classic Josephine the Plumber commercials won her a whole new set of fans. Jane is one of the few big names who cares about the movie history she helped to make. With nine rented warehouses and her own home overflowing, she is the Queen of the Collectors, a FOOF (Friend of Old Film) of the first rank. Even before she became Shirley Temple's rival, Jane was a movie nut who hung around Hollywood restaurants to snag the stars' autographs. She claims never to have thrown anything away, and she pursues relics that she wants regardless of their size—she has the 30-foot pirate galley from Tyrone Power's *The Black Swan* and the first set from *The Tonight Show.* Jane can't even estimate how much she has spent on her passion. "It's frightening, and I just hope I can keep affording to do it," she says. Jane hopes, as do her pals like Debbie Reynolds, that Hollywood will one day have a proper museum for the history that is so fast disappearing. Despite broken marriages and illnesses in her family, Jane has never lost her ingenuous enthusiasm. With an infectious giggle, she declares: "Hollywood, remember, is where dreams come true."

SHIRLEY TEMPLE

This child frightens me. She knows all the tricks. She backs me out of the camera, she blankets me, crabs my laughs —she's making a stooge out of me," groused Adolphe Menjou while making *Little Miss Marker* in 1934. He added, "She's Ethel Barrymore at six." Mae West had another opinion of the kid who was beating her at the box office. Shirley was nothing but a 50-year-old midget, declared Mae. By 1936 she was the greatest child star of all time. Lloyds of London insured her for millions but included a clause that no benefits would be paid if she met her death by intoxication. Deftly cast, Shirley was always reconciling irreconcilable foes through her warm-hearted innocence. No wonder the world doted on this child of a Los Angeles bank teller; she took the chill out of the gathering darkness from Europe.

"I don't see many movies—the language is so rough. Then when I catch something like *Paternity* on a plane, I'm afraid to laugh because everybody turns around and thinks, 'There's Shirley Temple laughing at a Burt Reynolds sex comedy.'" It's never been easy or less than a job being Shirley Temple. Visiting Smithfield, New Jersey, to help launch a Temple plate for the Norman Rockwell limited edition club, she explains, "I gave them a bad time here. I didn't like

the face, so I sent it back, and the hair's not right and it has blue eyes!" She throws up her hands and plops on some pillows on the floor for Horst. "They wanted me to do this promotion at the Playboy Casino in Atlantic City. Can you imagine me at a Playboy anything?" Shirley is wearing a formless "Boo-Boo," a native dress from Ghana, where she was the American ambassador in 1974–75. "Men carry sewing machines on their heads there and will stitch up anything while you wait. Of course, the women do 80 percent of the work in those coun-

tries—clear the fields, plant, harvest, not to mention having the children. I'm proud of my Ghana years." She was less happy about her stint as the first woman chief of protocol for the State Department under President Ford. "Too many people looked at you as if you were their maid. The wives of ambassadors who needed help with their hair, things like that." Though a Republican, she's not a Reaganite (they made *That Hagen Girl* together in 1947). "I disagree with him on many basics—ERA, détente, abortion. Women must have the right to make their own personal choices." Sworn in as a foreign affairs expert, Shirley has helped to train 88 diplomats,

but as for acting again . . . "Never, never, never. I don't have any interest after all the really interesting things I've done with my adult life. I even turned down a 'What Becomes a Legend Most' mink ad. I wouldn't feel comfortable with the state of our country by posing in a fur coat and being known as a rich Republican. Maybe they'll ask me again when the Democrats are back in the White House."

Shirley's second marriage, to Charles Black, a naval reserve officer when they married in 1950 and now a successful West Coast businessman, is a good one. Their three grown children aren't show business bound. "Well, my youngest daughter is kind of interested in rock and studies voice. But what child performers go through today! My mother would be spinning if she knew about those nude shots of Brooke Shields. And did you read that book by Joan Crawford's daughter? It may be true, but to write about your mother that way. Crawford once gave me a cocker spaniel; it was sick and had distemper and died the very next day. I never had the nerve to tell her!" Shirley has been working on her autobiography for years. "If I ever get past age 10, there's just too much to write. But this nostalgia craze amazes me. I made $10,000 just signing 2,000 limited Shirley Temple posters at $5 each. I told my husband that was the easiest money I ever made."

The snow is starting to fall in Smithfield. Shirley says she couldn't sleep the night before "in a big strange bed," a line she undoubtedly used many times before as Curly Top or Wee Willie Winkie or Madame Ambassador. As she bids goodbye, she adds, "I was so happy to meet you and have my picture taken, *and* I'm so sorry I've grown old for you."

DAME JUDITH ANDERSON

"Oh, God help you if she doesn't like you. She's simply a fiend in human form," offers a neighbor about Australia's greatest actress, Dame Judith Anderson. "And I hear she sleeps with her cats." Driving into the Anderson "ranch" in the hills above Santa Barbara, no cats are to be seen. The rather forbidding pseudo-French château, suitably dark enough for Mrs. Danvers in Hitchcock's *Rebecca*—Anderson's best-loved movie role—is echoing with the yapping of dachshunds. At the door stands Dame Judith, regal and cool, who scoops up one of the dogs. "Dachshunds have always been my favorite, but I'm afraid sex has reared its ugly head. Heidi-Ho is in heat." That grand Plantagenet profile has survived the years and fits marvelously into the gothic feel of the place. "We call it a ranch in this part of the world, and I bought it at the end of a second and *most* unhappy marriage." She breaks into a throaty chuckle, "when I did not know *one* thing about the fungi that go through our avocados here." Mrs. Danvers, Lady Scarface, Lady Macbeth, Medea—roles stamped as her own—does know how to laugh, and at herself too. "Act again? Did you say 'Act again?' Are you crazy? Have you checked *Who's Who* lately? (It reads: Frances Margaret Anderson, born February 10, 1898, Adelaide, Australia, daughter of the owner of a silver mine.) It is that dirty, dirty word, my dear—age." Then, striking a pose worthy of her high dramas, Dame Judith intones, "Medea, Medea, I shall not hear that music again."

Wrong. In 1982 Dame Judith returned to *Medea*, not in the title role that she commissioned her friend, the poet Robinson Jeffers, to create for her in the 1940s, but in the supporting role of the Nurse. She had seen another Australian on televi-sion and thought her perfect for the part. That actress, Zoe Caldwell, was married to Robert Whitehead, who had produced Anderson's production 30-odd years earlier; but they hadn't spoken in all those years due to Dame Judith's star temperament. She picked up the phone and buried the hatchet. Whitehead reciprocated by talking his original Medea into the comeback role, which earned her a Tony nomination. It also added a few notches to the Anderson backstage reputation. When Helen Hayes wanted to pay her respects one night, Dame Judith refused to see her. In a light-hearted book, Helen and Anita Loos had made fun of the Hamlet that Anderson had attempted with disastrous results in 1970. Then when *Rebecca* star Joan Fontaine let it be known she'd like to visit after a performance, Dame Judith gave in: "Well, I felt sorry for the poor thing, she is such a phony." Joan, though, had the last laugh; she didn't show up. *Medea*, it turned out, was not a swan song. Six months past her 85th birthday, Dame Judith signed for her first movie in 14 years, *Star Trek III: The Search for Spock.*

Dame Judith arrived in America with a letter of introduction to Cecil B. DeMille. He took one look at the 17-year-old and sent her packing to New York, where she did her long apprenticeship. By the time Queen Elizabeth II made her Dame of the British Empire in 1959, she had played most of the great classical parts (Gertrude to John Gielgud's Hamlet, Lady Macbeth to Maurice Evans's and Laurence Olivier's Macbeth) on both sides of the Atlantic. "If I've reached the top, then I've also hit the bottom more than I care to recall." In her personal life, bottom came when she was being wooed in Paris by producer Jed Harris, not knowing that Ruth Gordon was pregnant with his illegitimate son. Dame Judith slowly strokes her dachshund, conjuring up images of Mrs. Danvers standing behind Joan Fontaine counting 20 imaginary brush strokes. Heidi-Ho bolts and Dame Judith throws up her hands in mock frustration. "That dog is like her mistress. I have always said mine was never a serene temperament."

SUE CAROL

Her steps are measured, each sending a little echo through the rooms of a Bel Air mansion immaculately preserved in late 1950s modern. Slowly Sue Carol walks into view dressed in black, a Yorkie in her arms. She apologizes for the wait. "I hate being photographed and usually I turn down these things, but as I told you on the phone, I thought maybe I should take advantage of Mr. Horst, and then, who knows, time *is* passing." In her early 70s, Sue is prettier than the recent snapshots that occasionally appeared in the society pages of the Los Angeles and Palm Springs papers. Her chubby cheeks, an attribute turned trademark as with so many Jazz Age cuties, are amazingly unlined. Sue goes on to explain: "I have a congestive heart condition and my lungs fill up with fluid and I try to take it easy."

Within a year, and with only scant press coverage, she will succumb to this long illness. Little note was made that in her heyday Sue starred in over 25 movies, mostly musicals, and after being chosen a Wampas Baby Star in 1927 was considered something of a threat to that supreme jazz baby, Clara Bow. An "all-singing, all-dancing" flapper, Carol introduced "The Breakaway" in *Fox Movietone Follies* and inspired one of the great hits of the times, "Sweet Sue." Because Fox was so criminal in not preserving its early sound films, many Sue Carol musicals are lost and it is impos-

sible to judge what her popularity was based on. Her obituaries instead concentrated on Sue Carol starmaker, the agent who launched Peter Lawford, Rory Calhoun and Julie London; the ex-star who took a bit player and radio performer named Alan Ladd as her third husband and made him a heartthrob of the 1940s and a box office king into the 1950s; the dominating mother figure whose children and in-laws have made the Ladd legacy a force in today's film and television industry. Daughter Carol Lee Veitch is married to the former production president of Columbia Pictures, while her brother, the ex–child actor David Ladd, is now in independent production with his brother-in-law John Veitch. David's ex-wife is Cheryl Ladd. Younger daughter Alana Ladd gave up her teenage acting career and married West Coast talk show personality Michael Jackson. Alan Ladd, Jr., Sue's stepson from Alan Sr.'s first marriage, is acknowledged to be one of the half dozen most powerful (and nicest) men in Hollywood, the studio chief at 20th-Fox who okayed George Lucas's *Star Wars* and now heads up the Ladd Company. This all sits well with Sue, who disdained her own career. "My career, who cares? I never did, I never even liked acting."

Born Evelyn Lederer into a socially prominent Jewish family in Chicago, she was heiress to a real estate and brewery fortune started by her grandfather, sole distributor of Schenley whiskey in this country until he sold out to Joseph P. Kennedy, Sr. Moving west with her family, Sue was discovered in 1926 while visiting a movie set with a group of high school students. A decade later she took a walk, never to act again. Supposedly insulted while making a screen test, she knew she was too good for this "kind of slavery" and set up Sue Carol and Associates, an agency that became a Sunset Strip landmark. Her second, unhappy marriage to early sound star Nick Stuart fizzled (they co-starred in such ditties as *Why Leave Home, Girls Gone Wild, Chasing Through Europe* and *Secret Sinners*). But third husband Alan Ladd's overnight stardom after he appeared with Veronica Lake in Graham Greene's *This Gun for Hire* was one of the fastest rises of any personality of the World War II years and Sue's proudest achievement. However, she always downplayed her part and credited her husband's charisma, athletic ability and uniquely sexy voice. She also was modest about her dynamic dealings in real estate and the stock market. In Palm Springs alone you can find her gift shop and hardware store, the Ladd Spanish Inn and Sue Carol Interior Decorating.

In her later years, though, ill health was not the only dark cloud. Ladd's death in 1964 at age 50 from an accidental overdose of alcohol and barbiturates was crushing, and the later revelations in biographies and co-workers' autobiographies—tales of his fights with depression and drink and the extramarital affairs, primarily with June Allyson—were hard to deal with. But on the day of our photo session, Sue could talk of little more than "my Alan." Several times she repeated, "We were so much in love." She was pleased when we admired the magnificent ruby ring she was wearing. "Originally it was a drop from a necklace Alan bought for me years ago. But it was just too expensive and he didn't have the money at the time. So when I found out it cost $18,000 I had him take it back. But he secretly had the drop made into this ring. It's my favorite. Six months later, I heard the jeweler sold the necklace for $84,000 without the drop." Her voice becomes very quiet. "Alan always, *always* was doing things for me. He was that kind of loving man." Behind Sue Carol Ladd, as she preferred being called, is a picture of a beautiful blond idol from another generation. The inscription reads: "For you Susie—May we always be the 'complete unit' we are now. I love you so, Laddie."

CLAIRE TREVOR

Claire Trevor lights up a True and takes another sip of gin and orange. "I was never like Loretta Young. Now *that's* a movie star. When I made a film with her (*Second Honeymoon*), she had to be rolled out of her dressing room to the sound stage because she didn't allow a hair on her head out of place. I admired the way she sort of glided onto a set. Me? I just didn't care that much." Care or not, the Trevor talent willed out. After reigning as the Queen of the Bs at Fox in the 1930s, she did memorable free-lance work. Her Dallas, the saloon floozy kicked out of town in John Ford's *Stagecoach*, is the definitive whore with a heart of gold. Her Gaye, the dipso mistress of gangster Edward G. Robinson in John Huston's *Key Largo* in 1948, won her a supporting Oscar and added another decade to her Hollywood career. But a third marriage to tycoon Milton Bren, which lasted 30 years until his death in 1979, meant more to her than acting. "I simply had the greatest husband and I'll never stop missing him." Shortly after Bren's death, one of her sons was killed in a plane crash. To ease the pain, Claire moved from Newport Beach to a Fifth Avenue tower co-op in 1981 and got caught up in the Manhattan social whirl. She also made her first film in 20 years, *Kiss Me Goodbye*, a flop, though at 72 she never looked more glamorous. "I'm lucky I don't have to work, and while there are still a lot of things for me to do, keeping up my name is not one of them." Claire takes another drag on her cigarette and you know she means it.

LILLIAN GISH

The most important woman in the history of films is a die-hard Republican ("Well, I have to admit I voted for Roosevelt in 1936") and an Episcopalian—St. Bartholomew's on Park Avenue is her church ("I plan to be buried there with my mother and my sister Dorothy"). Like most actresses, Lillian is vain, and she tells Horst, "I like a high camera and a low light, and my hair always looks as if it's been combed by a bellows." She also lies about her age. She was born October 14 in either 1894 or 1896, but she much prefers "1899." Whatever the year, she remembers that the Gerry Society, an organization against child labor, was never far from the door when she and her sister toured in the first decade of this century. Friend Colleen Moore says, "Lillian may be our finest actress ever, but don't overlook the fact she was also our most desirable femme fatale— because she was so damned unattainable. Why, Colonel McCormick (of the Chicago newspaper empire) offered her the world, but she was married to her mother and her career."

The legend of Lillian rests on the achievement of a career unparalleled in theatrical history. No other star can rival her longevity. For over 80 years, she has acted in movies, theater, radio, television. She bore witness to the birth of an art form with its first master, D. W. Griffith, and she still bears witness to the power and importance of the movies, preferably silent ones, with her lec-

tures. Yet her work onstage—Ophelia to John Gielgud's Hamlet, the prostitute in Sean O'Casey's *Within the Gates*, Vinnie in *Life with Father*—showed even greater range. Today Lillian is universally acclaimed, and who could argue with a judgment made years ago. Richard Barthelmess, who co-starred in Griffith's *Way Down East*, once recalled the scene where Lillian had to float down a river on a cake of ice, often 20 times a day, for two weeks. Her face turned blue, icicles hung from her hair and eyelashes. "I was scared silly," he admitted, "but Lillian was superhuman. She lived in the spirit. There was never any other woman like her."

IRIS ADRIAN

Gum-chewing, wisecracking Iris Adrian is a Holly-wood institution. "What the hell do you mean by that?" screams the veteran of over 100 movies and nearly as many television shows. Born in 1912 in Los Angeles, Iris always sounded more like Brook-lyn with that fire-engine voice and either a bright blonde or red dye job to match. Give Iris a walk-on or toss her a real role—Two-Gun Gertie the mur-deress in Ginger Rogers's *Roxie Hart*—she would take the part and run with it. Jack Benny felt the force of her comic elbow in the ribs during the two decades she appeared on his radio and television series. She hasn't had a good role in years, but "Iris has no worries, Iris saved up like a smart dame," she confides, speaking of herself in the third person. She wraps a stuffed toy snake around her neck and yells at her husband, Fido Murphy, the ex-football pro, to feed a dozen or more stray cats who are quite literally sitting on chairs in the kitchen waiting for supper. "Animals are better than kids or actors any day." Iris lost Fido in 1983, but she says their 25 years together were "a hell of a lot better than if I'd gotten hitched to a damned actor. If an actor gets a pimple on his butt, he thinks he's ruined for life. They are so damned vain, it would be like marrying another dame!" She tosses the snake aside, tries on a hat and yells at Horst, "Kid, shoot it, I look gorgeous."

EVE ARDEN

Playing second fiddle to the great stars took a lot of fine tuning. Eve Arden was the virtuoso supreme at this specialty. Critic David Shipman said it best: "She was more eloquent than all the choruses of Euripides," and, it should be added, worth a lot more laughs. Eve says she never aspired to stardom; yet no matter what her billing, she was the star in the eyes of her fans. In the 1950s, bringing the radio series *Our Miss Brooks* to television, she almost challenged Lucille Ball in popularity, though she was much too manicured to do the wacky slapstick Lucy loved. "I saw so many unhappy stars, obsessed with themselves, I wanted more than that," Eve explains. "I wanted my own life, particularly my own family." With her second husband, the late Brooks West, she got her wish, creating a loving home for four children on a ranch that once was Ronald Colman's hideaway. Putting her career aside, she thought nothing of going off to Europe for a year and a half to show the kids another world, "to share that kind of experience." The balance worked and her career lasted too. With Woody Allen's *The Purple Rose of Cairo,* Eve is celebrating her 55th year in films. For such a homebody, it's ironic that her most famous line came in *Mildred Pierce,* describing Joan Crawford's scheming, murderous daughter played by Ann Blyth. "Alligators have the right idea, they eat their young."

JANET GAYNOR

Sitting under her painting of petunias, Janet Gaynor is all smiles. Her stock-in-trade has always been sunny-side up, the title of the 1929 musical she made at the height of her popularity as America's darling, dimpled child-woman. Her place in Hollywood history is a given: the first actress to win an Oscar in 1928 (for three films—*Seventh Heaven, Street Angel, Sunrise*); a reputation for being off-screen everything she was not on-screen, namely, a hard businesswoman; taking Adrian, the movie colony's premier designer, as her second husband; and, at 32, chucking it all after having made the big leap from Cinderella roles to mature parts such as her memorable Esther Blodgett in the first *A Star Is Born.* Her comebacks also made news, a weak Pat Boone vehicle called *Bernardine* in 1957 or, after years of inactivity, touring in *On Golden Pond* and doing *Harold and Maude* on Broadway. "And don't forget the nostalgia business," she says. "It's so booming I could be busy every night, telling about how Fay Wray used to pick me up in her Model T when Hollywood still had dirt roads." In September 1982, Janet and her third husband, the producer Paul Gregory, were in San Francisco to visit Janet's dearest friend, Mary Martin. A drunken driver in a speeding van hit the cab they were all riding in, wrapping it around a tree. Mary's manager Ben Washer was killed and Janet critically injured. She suffered a broken pelvis, collarbone and 11 ribs, ruptured her bladder and damaged her kidneys. At 77, it was doubtful she would survive. But four months and many operations later, Janet left the hospital for her Palm Springs home. Her husband sends out bulletins regularly: "She's so much better, she has even taught one of the burros on our place to share her Coca-Cola. She wants to do an ad—you don't have to be an ass to like Coke." On the day of our visit, Janet, in the wee voice that once sang "I'm a dreamer, aren't we all," confesses that old age "kind of creeps up on you, it happens so fast." Then she smiles, "But don't get me wrong, I do prefer it to the alternative."

JETTA GOUDAL

Cecil Beaton, in a rare lapse of judgment, may have dismissed her as "a passing exotic of Persian-cat perfection," but Jetta Goudal was the most alluring femme fatale in silent films; she was also the smartest, the best dressed (usually her own designs) and the feistiest. An overimaginative press agent put out the rumor that she was the daughter of Mata Hari, her lightly Gallic accent the proof. Today Jetta, ever mysterious, reveals nothing: "Just say I was born on the other side of the moon." Then taking a deep breath, as if the sky were about to fall, she divulges, "The great sorrow of my life is that I was not born blonde. With my blue eyes, it is a tragedy." Jetta has been wheeled into the living room of her antique-rich Los Angeles apartment by a nurse-companion. "You've heard of Mae West, meet May East." With that, Jetta and May go at each other like a vaudeville team. "I must have the right gloves, put them out, I have to see all of them, I shall not be photographed without the right, the best gloves, for this genius photographer." May groans; she's pooped from laying out all the dresses. "This is her favorite dress, I think. Today it's her favorite anyway. We had to buy two of them, and I sewed them together to make a fit." Wounded, Jetta

weakly confesses, "I love good chocolates and, well, I've put on weight, ever since my accident. I always took care of my figure, and now to come to this!" Stricken with a "delicate heart" years ago, she later tripped over a phone cord, never to recover after extensive surgery. But the Goudal reputation was that of a fighter and remains so today. "I started taking medicine, but my God, it wrecked my skin. I was never a beauty, I admit that, but I had a presence. My hair, my hands were beautiful. I was tops."

Jetta's best work is in C. B. DeMille's 1925 *The Road to Yesterday*, playing a dual role as a frigid modern wife who is reincarnated as a passionate gypsy; D. W. Griffith's *Lady of the Pavements*, as a countess spurned by her fiancé, who trains a prostitute to be his bride; and *White Gold*, totally out of her vamp characters playing the bride of a sheepman in this little-known 1927 masterpiece. She lost an important role that might have made her a bigger name: Diane in *Seventh Heaven*. "DeMille would not release me for *Heaven*—he was offered 10 times my contract salary, and they cast Janet Gaynor (who won the first Oscar as best actress). She is a stupid woman, no wonder Charlie Farrell got all the close-ups. You can't show intelligence in a close-up and he was prettier too." Jetta sued DeMille the next year and won an important case. Historian DeWitt Bodeen believes "all

actors owe Jetta their gratitude for going to court to establish a star's rights." She also became known as the Joan of Arc of Equity when she fought for the formation of the Screen Actors Guild as a branch of Actors Equity, which the studios opposed. None of this helped her career. Then, though her voice was as sultry as her looks, fashions changed with the arrival of sound. Her swan song in 1932 was *Business and Pleasure*—a continental femme fatale, she chased Will Rogers.

Jetta married one of the best of the Hollywood scenic designers, Harold Grieve, and for 50 years they have been a vital part of the cultural if not the movie scene in Los Angeles, with her husband turning to interior design and the fine arts. Finally she has selected the proper gloves, put on her furs with hat to match—"Hats are lifesavers, you know." Jetta wants to stand for the picture, though it will pain her. "I don't like the fake. Never have. Always say it's got to be real sable or nothing at all. Yes, there's one last request: I don't like being called a silent star. Who was silent? I was *never* silent!"

EVELYN LAYE

Any old theater buff can tell you about *Helen!* This shimmering but short-lived opéra bouffe about the Trojan War, based on Offenbach's *La Belle Hélène*, cast its glow over a Depression London in early 1932. To this day it bedevils the memory of those who came under its spell. Directed by that renowned exponent of stage spectacle, Professor Max Reinhardt, it had music by Erich Wolfgang Korngold, dances by Léonide Massine and scenic design and costumes by Oliver Messel said to be so revolutionary they ushered in white as the color for the "moderne" decade ahead. But most of all, *Helen!* had Evelyn Laye. She had returned to London from New York where she "electrified" Broadway in Noel Coward's *Bitter Sweet*—one critic said, "She puts a heavy tax on superlatives"—and from Hollywood where she made a not-so-happy debut for Sam Goldwyn in *One Heavenly Night.* But in *Helen!* she was a divine vision in white. In the boudoir scene, her blonde hair was the only touch of color in a blindingly white setting—white circular bed, dozens of white pillows, white palm trees (actually the bedposts), white swans. For the finale, all Evelyn had to do was appear atop the walls of Troy, and both Greek and Trojan armies put down their arms to sing her praises.

Born in 1900 of theatrical parents, Evelyn, or "Boo" as she has been called from her first utterance, made her debut at four and by 1923 was a

London headliner in a revival of *The Merry Widow*. *Lilac Time*, *Blue Eyes*, *The New Moon* were among her biggest West End hits. Having turned down Noel Coward when he wanted her for *Bitter Sweet* in London, she later made up for the mistake by doing it on Broadway. Percy Hammond, then dean of the New York critics, raved: "She is the loveliest prima donna this side of heaven." Fifty years later, on a wintry day in late 1981, Evelyn is at the Algonquin Hotel in New York in a suite often used by Coward. Reputedly one star who really lived the star part outside as well as inside the theater, even when her fame faded after World War II, Evelyn is no prima donna, just full of the devil. "They want me to sing a few of Noel's songs in a tribute downstairs, that's why I'm over here." She stops short. "Now Noel, behave yourself. Did you see that? He moved that vase. He did it this morning too. I know you are in the room, dear Noel, but please do behave yourself, we have company." She winks, then goes back to the conversation with her long departed friend and colleague. "I really don't believe I believe in death—really. Why, my husband (the late actor Frank Lawton) came back to me one night. I sleep on my right side, you see, and he whispered in my left ear, even sang a bit of our favorite song." Evelyn is laughing gaily. "Oh, do forgive me, I was good about 50 years ago." That was when two continents were in love with her and Sigmund Romberg and Oscar Hammerstein II were inspired to write a song for Evelyn in *The Night Is Young* aptly called "When I Grow Too Old to Dream (I'll Have You to Remember)."

BARBARA STANWYCK

In *Baby Face,* Barbara Stanwyck plays a mantrap cut from common clay, her screen persona in the early 1930s. When she throws open the window of her Erie, Pennsylvania, shanty in the opening scene and blows the soot off the geraniums in the window box, there's no question Barbara has got to be reckoned with. In those days she also was striking a blow for every working girl who had her own nose pressed against the window pane but came to the movies to escape. For the male moviegoer, she had even more to offer. Often shopworn but usually sincere, she was an earthy temptress, the variety that screenwriter Herman Mankiewicz defined as "ideal." He wrote, "I dream of being married to her and living in a little cottage in Beverly Hills. I'd come home from a hard day at MGM and Barbara would be there to greet me with an apple pie she had cooked herself . . . and wearing no panties."

Upgrading her image in the 1940s, Barbara landed better scripts. The blue-collar days were over, but she remembered all the tricks of the trade and still got her way. In Preston Sturges's *The Lady Eve,* playing a cardsharpy vamp who passes for an English lady, Barbara creates a deliciously cunning character. Her victim is a gullible herpetologist named Hopsy Pike (Henry Fonda), who gasps: "You're certainly a funny girl for anyone to meet who's been up the Amazon for a year." Barbara's other great role around this period was the deadly, peroxided Phyllis Dietrichson in Billy Wilder's chilling *Double Indemnity,* in which she ensnares a weakling (Fred MacMurray) in a scheme to knock off her husband and collect the insurance. These roles, the light side and the dark of the American breed of desirable femme fatale, demonstrate what critic Richard Corliss said: "When she was good, she was very, very good. And when she was bad, she was terrific."

This self-made star calls herself "a tough old dame from Brooklyn." She began life in 1907 as Ruby Stevens, the youngest of five children. She lost her mother when she was two, and her father, a bricklayer, deserted his family two years later. Ruby knew four or five foster homes before she was 10, though sister Mildred, a show girl, looked after her when she wasn't touring. Mildred's boyfriend, James "Buck" Mack of the vaudeville team of Miller and Mack, taught little Ruby how to dance. (He lived with Barbara into the 1950s.) By 13, she had eluded the truant officers and was working full-time—store clerk, receptionist at *Vogue,* a stint at the phone company. Lying about her age, Ruby was soon dancing at the Strand Roof. She rode an elephant in the 1922 Ziegfeld Follies, and during those "cold-water flat" days one producer gave her some good advice: "Go to the zoo and watch how the animals move." Legend has it that Ruby studied the panther with its long, powerful stride. The Stanwyck walk, authoritative and assured, would become a trademark. The big chance came on Broadway in *The Noose,* followed by her silent film debut in *Broadway Nights,* and then a personal triumph in *Burlesque* in 1927. If

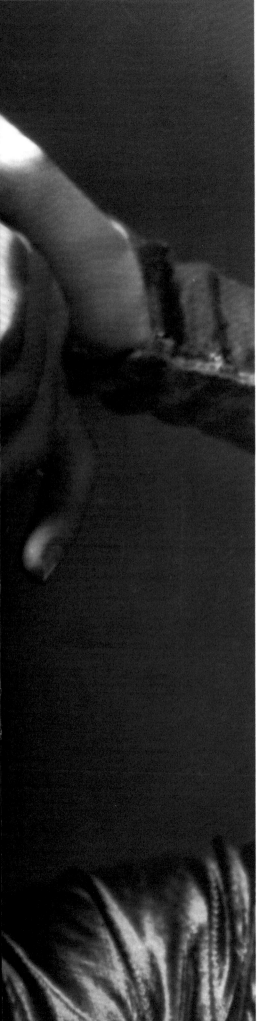

she had not met and married Frank Fay, the comedian who was on his short-lived stardom kick in the movies, Barbara might have been a major stage actress. Instead, she followed Fay to Hollywood, where the worst happened. His career nose-dived, hers skyrocketed. Fay became a drunk, they fought often and openly in public, went through an ugly divorce and custody battle over an adopted son. (Barbara has not seen her son in over 30 years.)

Just as the theater was the salvation of her unhappy childhood, the movies became a refuge during those bleak days. A workaholic, Barbara existed only on the sound stage, her friends the crew and technicians. When she fell in love with Robert Taylor in 1936, it looked as if personal happiness was at hand. For a while it was. But when they divorced in 1952, Barbara retreated into her work again and made six films in a year. She also fell in love with Robert Wagner while making *Titanic*, but a 23-year age difference sank this romance. In print Hedda Hopper accused her of being a bitter recluse, while Barbara herself faced the years frankly. "When an actress reaches a certain age, then she's got to know where she stands." But television during the 1960s and her four-year run in *The Big Valley* brought the Stanwyck personality to a new generation of fans. Her last success was winning the Emmy for best actress in 1983 for her role in *The Thorn Birds* as the matriarch who lusts after priest Richard Chamberlain. Picking up her award, she singled out Ann-Margret in *Who Will Love My Children* as more deserving of the Emmy that year.

In 1982, when the Film Society of Lincoln Center honored her, Barbara confessed she thought they had made a mistake and wanted Barbra Streisand. Frank Capra, who directed Barbara in five films starting with her first movie hit, *Ladies of Leisure*, told the 2,500 guests, "It's this gift of hers to communicate the truth of a role which has made Barbara the great actress she is. She's played them all—big-city dames and cattle queens, adulterous wives and dewy-eyed ingenues. Her many faces are all different, and all dazzling." Earlier that same day at the photo session with Horst, this shy star said she wanted only one thing. "It would be nice to work as long as I can. I always said I was never much for hobbies."

LYNN FONTANNE

Isn't it lovely. It fetches you up!" Lynn Fontanne, admitting to 92 but probably closer to 95, is serving tea in the little sitting room off the parlor of the "magical" home, Ten Chimneys, that she and Alfred Lunt made for themselves in Genesee Depot, Wisconsin. Alfred modeled the house on a Finnish farm with a two-story living room surrounded by a balcony. It's a cool September day, and this just may be the last formal photo sitting for the lady of the house. Lynn excuses herself to put on "a Valentina. I've held onto all my Valentinas. They're always in style," she whispers as she exits the tea party. George Bugbee, the widower of Alfred's sister, is playing host. "Can you believe that Lynn rides her exercise bike for 30 minutes every day and insists on her scotch and water, no ice, every night before dinner. This woman is so disciplined Alfred used to complain it took her forever to get to bed. It seems someone years ago told her to use 22 toothbrushes—dry—and she still does, and she still has her teeth." Lynn returns, gloriously gowned. "This dress may go back to 1937, oh, maybe just 1947, but I'm so happy I can wear it for you." She starts to reminisce about visiting backstage in London with her mentor, the legendary Ellen Terry, and being introduced to Ellen's very stiff young nephew, making his stage debut. "He was John Gielgud." Then, quite pleased with herself, she says, "Tell me my face doesn't look like those walnut faces I see in the papers. I don't know why I've

been allowed to keep my age so well, because 92 is a very big age."

On July 30, 1983, Lynn Fontanne died. Bugbee made the announcement. "Lynn just wilted away. I don't suppose the weather helped. We're having a heat wave." In the fall a memorial service was held on Broadway at the Lunt-Fontanne Theatre. It was a joyous affair, and slanted toward the domestic Lunts rather than the accomplishments of the greatest acting team in the history of the theater. Producer Charles Bowden remembered how Alfred always cooked and Lynn always dressed the house. "He'd thin out the carrot patch with tweezers to get the straightest, sweetest carrots in the country." Bowden also told of their Jersey cow named Ellen Terry "because she was so smooth and round" and how Lynn interfered when Alfred wanted to send the animal out for artificial insemination. "She's had little enough pleasure in life," Lynn stated, and off the cow went for a week with a bull. Their friend and lawyer Donald Sewell recalled that the last time Alfred and Lynn came to Broadway in 1970 they went to see *Home.* When they entered the theater, the audience rose and applauded. "There must be someone important here—everyone's standing," Alfred told Lynn. After his death in 1977, says Sewell, "Lynn never shed a tear, not then, not ever. She had courage. Once she did ask me, 'Was I really Alfred's equal?' I assured her, 'Of course, or you never would have been the Lunts.' Lynn smiled and said, 'Then I'm glad for Alfred's sake.'"

JANE RUSSELL

When Howard Hughes's publicist Russell Birdwell went to work on a Bible-reading, 19-year-old ex-tomboy named Ernestine Jane Russell, a new but not glorious chapter was logged in the making of a celebrity and the exploitation of the female. Hughes's discovery, with a deadpan worthy of Buster Keaton, tended to suffer her fate lightly. As conceived by Hollywood's master glamour photographer, George Hurrell, Jane's initial pinups showed her sucking on a straw in a haystack, wearing a low-cut peasant blouse. The tag lines read: "Mean, Moody, Magnificent" and "How Would You Like to Tussle with Russell?" Alaska named two peaks in her honor, and Bob Hope wasn't above introducing her with, "Here comes the two and only Jane Russell." In Baltimore, a judge upheld an idiotic Maryland censorship-decency case against her notorious, and notoriously bad, first movie, *The Outlaw.* He declared: "Miss Russell's breasts hung over the picture like a thunderstorm over a landscape. They were everywhere." In San Francisco, another judge handed down an acquittal, telling the jury: "We have seen Jane Russell. She is an attractive specimen of American womanhood. God made her what she is." The flackery, the controversy, the long-term contract with Hughes made Jane famous, rich and a household joke.

Today she is still making the most of her assets, pitching Playtex 18-hour real support bras for "us full-figured gals." Several years ago, when she hit a truck and refused an alcohol-level test, she says she expected headlines like "Jane Russell busted while in her cups." Jokes she can live with, but the lack of respect for her legitimate attributes is more difficult. It took time, but Jane developed into a superb straight woman for Hope and Groucho Marx, even Marilyn Monroe. In *Gentlemen Prefer Blondes,* Jane did a mean takeoff on her co-star, impersonating Marilyn in the courtroom sequence, something Marilyn could never have brought off if the roles had been reversed. Jane has a good voice too. In *The Las Vegas Story* she did a terrific job on Hoagy Carmichael's "I Get Along Without You Very Well," and when she replaced Elaine Stritch in Stephen Sondheim's *Company* on Broadway, she packed quite a wallop delivering "The Ladies Who Lunch." Financially sound and married to an Arizona real estate man (she divorced the late football star Bob Waterfield after 23 years and was widowed three months into her second marriage), Jane is tireless in her efforts for WAIF, the international organization devoted to placing foreign orphans with American families, which she founded in 1951. Her three children are adopted, and daughter Tracy presented Jane with twin granddaughters in 1983. But being a grandmother has not stopped the questions about what it's like being a sex symbol. Jane always gives the same answer: "Just a pain in the ass."

Filling out a passport form, Ann Miller in all seriousness listed her profession as "star." Stardom comes in degrees, hits in waves, and these four actresses run the gamut. They're all stars, past or present, or both. They've all had good years, known some bad ones.

June Haver, a kid performer and band soloist who was signed by 20th Century-Fox as a teenage threat to Betty Grable, eventually turned her back on $2,500-a-week stardom and got herself to a nunnery. Unhappy in both career and personal life, she wanted out that badly.

Seven months later she walked out of the convent, too, but by 1955 she had discovered permanent happiness as the second wife of widower Fred Mac-Murray. Married to one of Hollywood's richest actors (Fred has a reputation for watching every penny), June gives her time to working with battered children. At home Fred hooks rugs and bakes bread while June does needlepoint, swearing she'll never act again "ever."

Anne Jeffreys devotes much time to SHARE, the big Los Angeles show biz charity, but she hasn't abandoned her career, though at times it seemed it had abandoned her. She's always playing *The King and I* or *Kismet* or *The Sound of Music* on a stage somewhere, but the movies never did right by her creamy beauty and musical gifts. Anne's finest moment came in 1947 on Broadway as the star of Kurt Weill's opera *Street Scene,* and her one claim to popularity happened on the small screen doing the *Topper* series with her husband, Robert Sterling, in the 1950s.

"Older people don't have a place in television and movies," laments another beauty, Virginia Mayo. "They just sort of discard you after a certain age." The former Goldwyn bombshell who co-starred twice with Ronald Reagan lives in Thousand Oaks with her daughter, three grandchildren, two cats, one dog and an old Jaguar in the garage. Rightfully bitter, she speaks her mind. "It was the greatest thrill of my life to be in pictures. I'm not retired, it's just that la-

JUNE HAVER

ANNE JEFFREYS

dies get old, and unlike the older male stars, we just don't get the offers." Then she adds, "And I don't have to keep my name before the public by writing all that junk like some of my contemporaries," referring to the confessionals penned by her peers. "I had one husband and a happy, happy life with him," Virginia says about the late Michael O'Shea. In 1948, a year after their marriage, an Arab sheikh wrote to Virginia: "You're the surest proof to me of the existence of God." Today she

wonders, mockingly, "Where is that old sheikh when I need him the most."

Ann Miller has had a few sheikhs as well as other rich suitors in her life, but nowadays reveals, "I'm not happy not working and all three of my husbands wanted me to stop performing." This dervish of dancers, whose machine-gun tapping at 500 taps a minute is supposedly the world's record, has been a campy cutup since her debut in *New*

Faces of 1937. But even the days at MGM in the late 1940s and early 1950s—she got her best notices in the film version of *Kiss Me Kate,* strutting her stuff in "Too Darn Hot" in 3-D—never brought the acclaim that awaited her 1979 arrival on Broadway in *Sugar Babies* with Mickey Rooney. She held her own with that scene-stealer ("I'm competitive and go out to win every performance") and proved for all time that her belting was as riveting as her dancing. It was not her singing, though, that got Ann the nickname "Miss Lips." "I have hoofer's

mouth disease," she says about the glib Millerisms. When asked if she would like to see a play called *The Trial of Lizzie Borden,* she declined on the grounds, "Who wants to see a show about a cow."

The more level-headed Virginia Mayo, after a play she did in Los Angeles in 1984 flopped, confessed, "I know the difference between fantasy and reality. You can live out your fantasies in the movies or on the stage, but just don't try to bring them home with you." A good rule for any star, any age, any time.

VIRGINIA MAYO

ANN MILLER

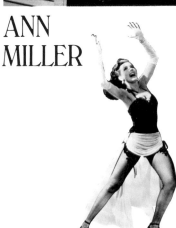

CYD CHARISSE

In the "Broadway Rhythm" number in *Singin' in the Rain*, Gene Kelly is a hick from the sticks adrift on the Great White Way. Neon flashing, he executes an amazing knee-slide, landing at the outstretched foot of a femme fatale. Kelly's hat dangles from the toe of her green satin slipper. The camera pans up the most spectacularly long leg to a close-up of the sultry sneer on the face of Cyd Charisse. Smoke is pouring out of her nostrils. It's a breathtaking moment—and movie musicals, as well as Cyd's career, would never be the same. At MGM since 1945, she had done all right as a featured or specialty player (*The Harvey Girls, Words and Music, The Kissing Bandit*), but after *Singin' in the Rain* in 1952, Cyd was the new queen of the musical, the dream dancer to partner Kelly (*Brigadoon, It's Always Fair Weather, Invitation to the Dance*) and Fred Astaire (*The Band Wagon, Silk Stockings*) into their twilight years. She closed out the golden age of classic Hollywood musicals.

"I've just returned from opening four department stores in Pennsylvania," Cyd says, standing on the edge of her patio wall overlooking Beverly Hills. This kind of promotion work pays well, and the fans, particularly the middle-aged women, clamor about to check out how little Cyd has aged. She tours constantly, too, in straight comedies (*Cactus Flower, Bell, Book and Candle*) and occasionally she works as a musical duo on the nightclub circuit or on a television special with her husband, the singer Tony Martin. All this keeps Cyd on her toes, figuratively if not literally. She is nowhere near calling it a day.

"I've done everything now but Broadway, and maybe it's not too late to believe that might happen yet. People forget that I always acted too. That's why *Silk Stockings* (the Cole Porter musical based on the Garbo-Lubitsch *Ninotchka*) is my favorite movie. I danced *and* acted in that one." Martin emerges from the wine cellar with champagne to celebrate the picture snapping. They have been married since 1948; his first wife was Alice Faye, her first husband dance instructor Nico Charisse.

Cyd was born Tula Ellice Finklea in Amarillo, Texas, in 1921 and by 14 was dancing with the Ballet Russe. "I still take classes every morning, ballet classes. That's why I still weigh 116." Cyd could pass for 40, and every move she makes is lighter than air. Floating to the baby grand with its autographed photos of Nixon, Kissinger, Johnson, JFK, she picks up an oversize book. "This is what I'm proud of," she says, displaying a lavishly illustrated homage published in French by a Parisian fan. "They tell me I'm big in France. I always did get loads of fan mail from there." But Cyd isn't particularly nostalgic. "Well, it was all hard work, hours upon hours. It took us months to do those things at MGM. But we did them right, didn't we?" Astaire paid her the ultimate compliment: "That Cyd. When you've danced with her, you stay danced with."

GENEVIEVE TOBIN

In their heyday, Genevieve Tobin and her husband, the director William Keighley, were rich and cultured and well traveled. Her sly brand of coquetry had conquered both Broadway and London's West End by the time the 1920s roared their last. Hollywood bound, she bade farewell to the stage in 1929 by introducing Cole Porter's "You Do Something to Me" in *Fifty Million Frenchmen*. In the 1930s, while Keighley was on the Warner Bros. assembly line directing James Cagney, Edward G. Robinson and Errol Flynn, Genevieve was making eyes at Maurice Chevalier in *One Hour with You*, being menaced by Humphrey Bogart in *The Petrified Forest* and waxing hysterical as the soubrette rival of Claudette Colbert in *Zaza*. Once they married in 1938—her first, his third—she quietly curtailed the acting jobs, retiring in 1941 at her husband's request. It would be nice to report they lived happily ever after. For a while they did—rather grandly. During World War II Keighley headed up the Army Air Forces Motion Picture Division and Genevieve was the toast of Washington, D.C. He hosted the popular Lux Radio Theatre, but never once asked his wife to appear. Retiring in the mid-1950s, Keighley devoted the next 15 years to photographing art treasures in Europe, and from their

home on the Avenue Foch, they were gay, giddy American expatriates. His slides of Mont-Saint-Michel and Versailles are in the collection of the Metropolitan Museum of Art. But illness came with the 1970s, and when we appeared at their Fifth Avenue apartment, Genevieve had forgotten the appointment. "She doesn't remember much," explained the maid in broken English, her baby crawling around the Keighley home. In the bedroom was Keighley, a victim of a stroke.

"What can I wear? I don't have any false eyelashes, and I didn't get my hair done. Does it look all right?" Genevieve rambled, a frail little bird fluttering around the cage of old age. "Here, this, can I wear this? It's pure silk, and I got it on our honeymoon in China. Oh, our honeymoon was wonderful. We went around the world, took us months and months." She has found a magnificent gold lamé robe in the disheveled closet. "I had so many beautiful things, and my jewelry, where has it all gone? Mr. Keighley could do anything. He designed this necklace in gold with lots of sapphires." She is terribly nervous, but as Horst prepares the lights, she lights up too. "I've lied about my age so much, please don't ask me how old I am—I don't know." She was born in 1901.

Keighley, though infirm, is lucid: "I'm in bad shape, but I have everything in trust for my little girl." He opens a drawer and pulls out a $788,000 trust fund certificate from Morgan Guaranty Trust. "She has been everything to me. I wish young people could have seen her onstage. There was never a more delightful comedienne, my lovely, adorable Genevieve." She chirps, "Now who else are you shooting? Claudette? Oh, do give her our love. Bette? Oh, amazing. AA, you know." Then Genevieve points to the wall. "There, that's our prize. We sold the Chinese antiques and all the silver at auction, but we'll never get rid of this." It is the Ordre National de la Legion d'Honneur given Keighley in 1961 for his documentation of the cathedrals and châteaux of France. "And when we are gone (he died in June, 1984), the Met is going to have a special collection called the William and Genevieve Tobin Keighley Library." She pats her husband's hand. "Not bad for the stepson of a Philly fireman and a poor Irish lass from 34th Street."

VERA HRUBA RALSTON

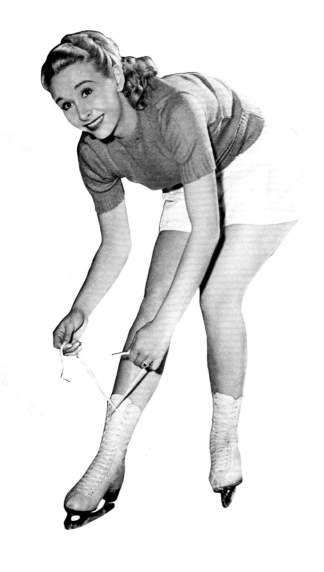

In the 1936 Olympics in Germany, a 15-year-old blonde ice skater from Czechoslovakia lost to Sonja Henie but won the silver medal and the eye of Hitler. Summoned to his box "by big storm troopers," Vera Hruba Ralston faced off with der Führer, plus Göring and Goebbels. Hitler suggested she might like to skate under the German flag. Her knees "trembling like Jello," Vera responded, "I'm very happy under my own flag. Once a Czech, always a Czech." Two years later she and her mother fled to England, then on to the United States, where she did the only thing she knew how to do—skate. Touring the Midwest in the Ice Capades, she caught the eye of another important and powerful man, Herbert Yates, a self-made, tough-minded millionaire who had worked his way up from newsboy to head of the American Tobacco Company. In 1935 he brought together a group of minor movie companies to form Republic Pictures, a factory for westerns, B melodramas and Judy Canova hillbilly comedies. With Yates as her mentor, Vera managed to trade in her skates to become Empress of Republic and eventually the wife of the Emperor himself. Though her fame and fortune never rivaled Henie's ("My God," Vera recalls, "she was unique, she could hold an audience by just standing still in a spotlight"), Vera was a young woman determined to do her best to be a star. She took acting lessons from Josephine Dillon, Clark Gable's first wife and coach. She may have been Yates's private property, but she never got high and mighty with her fellow players or the crews; everybody on the lot liked her. John Wayne reportedly considered her a good luck charm after he broke into the big money with his own production deals at Republic. Unfortunately, her movies made money only when she co-starred with Wayne. Vera never acted as well as she skated, and lacking top directors, writers and cameramen, she never had the quality backup that could make a difference for a neophyte. The titles of her 27 Republic productions tell the tale: *The Lady and the Monster, Storm Over Lisbon, Angel on the Amazon, Belle Le Grand, Spoilers of the Forest.* When Yates lost control of the studio, they retired to quiet splendor in Santa Barbara (at one time, they had homes in Los Angeles, Manhattan and on Long Island). Widowed in 1966, Vera today is slimmer and more relaxed than anytime during her acting days. With an adoring second, and younger, husband, Charles Alva, she herself seems to have dropped 20 years. They maintain the magnificent Pacific coastline estate in Santa Barbara, where they grow avocados, enjoy lots of exercise and swimming, and go off for almost daily hospital volunteer work. But what about the Vera Hruba Ralston cult that continues to bring fan mail and requests for personal appearances? "It is fun to look back sometimes, but I never felt so good in my whole life as I do now. Charlie keeps me in shape, I guess, and, hell, I am a happy woman." Her words are still faintly accented with an Eastern European flavor, and on the wall of her dining room, near the wedding silver John Wayne gave her, are the skates she wore in 1936.

LEATRICE JOY

Daughter: "I had to take her roller skates away from her last summer."

Mother: "Well, I'm not doing so bad. I am 87."

Vitality was always Leatrice Joy's secret weapon and she used it like a champ. She still does. "Here in Riverside (Connecticut), I'm a big fish in a small pond," she laughs, "and I love it." As the local celebrity, she is public-spirited ("I'll go around telling old folks to put a song in their hearts"), full of stories, mostly humorous ("There's nothing like a good joke!"), and quite indefatigable ("Of course, when you get old you got to get resourceful"). Leatrice was never less than resourceful. On the front porch of her little waterfront cottage—Tom Sawyer's Aunt Polly would feel at home here—there's an old ornate iron bench with "Leatrice Joy" carved into the back. "For 17 years this was at the corner of Hollywood Boulevard and Las Palmas," she explains. "All us stars back then had our names on the bus benches. When I heard that Los Angeles was getting rid of them, I just went right down and picked up mine off the street for myself. Which has held up better, me or the bench?"

Born and reared in New Orleans, Leatrice and her mother headed to New York

City when her father, a dentist, died of consumption. She gave herself six months to make good as a model and actress. She had had a little acting experience in school ("It gave me a wonderful feeling pretending to be someone else") and even made her movie debut locally for a Louisiana film outfit that went bankrupt ("I swear it wasn't my fault!"). With her personality as bright as the Fourth of July, Leatrice was an easy extra to spot in support of Alice Brady and Mary Pickford. "It's no secret," she says, "that when you come from the South you start with a little something extra." During the 1920s Leatrice breezed through Hollywood with freshness and gusto. Looking for a replacement for Gloria Swanson in his sophisticated bedroom-biblical melodramas, Cecil B. DeMille took Leatrice away from Sam Goldwyn but had no luck casting her in the Swanson mold. In two of DeMille's biggest hits, *Manslaughter* and the first *Ten Commandments,* in 1922 and 1923, Leatrice developed her own persona representing the new "modern" woman—upper-crust, a bit spoiled, but decidedly independent. In *The Clinging Vine* and *For Alimony Only* she went further, playing businesswomen with little time for love, precursors of the tweedy types later associated with Rosalind Russell. Cropping her hair short and styling it like a boy's, dressed by Hollywood's greatest designers, Adrian and Travis Banton, Leatrice became an international trendsetter. "My definition of a fashionable woman is one who wears the latest," she says, "but a stylish woman is one who bends the fashion. That's what I tried to do and I had wonderful help. Adrian was so creative. He took advantage of your disadvantages. Big shoulders make your waist look smaller, he always said." Neither flapper nor vamp, Leatrice was an original. She could have continued into the sound era—her voice has more than a tinge of southern drawl. "But I retired at my height. I could never see myself getting old on the screen." Over the years she *was* lured off the golf course

(her favorite sport) for a couple of movie parts and some stage work in stock. None of this approached a real comeback.

Still, there is more to the Leatrice Joy story. In 1921 she married John Gilbert on the eve of his reign as Hollywood's "Great Lover." Their romance, an early chapter in this Casanova's conquest of the most beautiful women of his generation, is legend. Movie historian and screenwriter DeWitt Bodeen thinks their love story could have been, should have been, written by F. Scott Fitzgerald—the fun-loving southern belle losing her heart forever to a lady killer who can't control his passion, can't reform, becomes alcoholic and suicidal. As it happened, sparks didn't fly when Leatrice and John first met. It took several films and three or four years, then a chance meeting before they really fell in love. They eloped to Mexico, and Leatrice remembers a mariachi combo strumming "Alexander's Ragtime Band" as their wedding music. She also recalls Gilbert tossing away the diamond wedding ring when she casually told him a plain gold one like her mother's would have been just fine. What followed were three years of separations and reconciliations. Leatrice was willing to give up her career and did announce retirement when their daughter was born in 1924. But within a year they were divorced and Gilbert was about to discover Garbo.

Even with two later marriages, Leatrice's love for Gilbert remains inviolate. She swears he was the only man "I truly, truly loved, and I'm just grateful to be the mother of his daughter." For years their daughter has researched a biography of her father, but she has received little or no cooperation from Garbo or his other wives, Ina Claire and Virginia Bruce. Gilbert once told screenwriter Lenore Coffee that "Leatrice is the only woman with whom I ever found peace." Today the nameplate on her fence reads "Gilbert." And Leatrice weeps when she recalls an inscription he wrote to her: "After whom God patterned the Angels."

MARY MARTIN

When Eddie Cantor was asked who Broadway's greatest musical star was, he thought, and then with due respect to the unique, phenomenal Ethel Merman, he answered, "Mary Martin." His reasoning made sense. Mary could play Ethel's roles (and did on tour in *Annie Get Your Gun*) but could anybody see Ethel as Nellie Forbush in *South Pacific* or as the postulant in *The Sound of Music* or flying as Peter Pan? Mary was a little lost lamb from Weatherford, Texas, trying to break into the big time when she got a chance in Cole Porter's *Leave It to Me* in 1938. Her naive three-minute strip to "My Heart Belongs to Daddy" in a cutoff lynx coat was one of the legendary showstoppers. By the time she made her Broadway musical farewell in 1966 as the eternal wife and mother figure in *I Do, I Do,* Mary may not have introduced as many classic songs as The Merm did in shows by Berlin, Gershwin, Porter and Styne, but she left no argument as to who was the warmest, most womanly of all our musical actresses. Mary not only gave her heart to Daddy but to the Broadway musical stage during its richest, most fruitful years.

FRANCES DEE

The ingenue is an endangered species, but one of the pleasures of moviegoing in the 1930s was the beguiling bevy of light hearted, doe-eyed young things who rarely got top billing yet always came through as an added treat. Jean Parker, Rochelle Hudson and Madge Evans were delectable. Then there was Frances Dee. A true beauty, she was radiant. Whether playing an uppity rich girl in *An American Tragedy* (the role Liz Taylor did in the remake, *A Place in the Sun*) or Meg to Katharine Hepburn's Jo in the 1933 *Little Women,* Frances was a versatile original. Critic James Agee noted she was "one of the very few women in movies who really had a face." Los Angeles-born and Chicago-reared, she worked as an extra before being hand-picked by Maurice Chevalier to be his leading lady in *Playboy of Paris* in 1930. In the next 10 years, she made 30 films, playing a wide range, from a virtuous Amelia Sedley in *Becky Sharp* to a masochistic deb in *Blood Money,* from a small-town sweepstake winner living it up in *The Gay Deception* to the regal Katherine DeVaucelles opposite Ronald Colman's François Villon in *If I Were King.* Her talent put her in the running for Scarlett O'Hara, too, and she continued to act until a change-of-life baby, her third son, came along in 1955. But to hear Frances tell it, the real accomplishment is her 50-year marriage to Joel McCrea, who, like his wife, is one of the most underrated of all screen performers. They met making *The Silver Cord* in 1933. In retrospect, his work in over 80 movies puts McCrea in the rare company of our best natural actors. In three major films by Preston Sturges (*Sullivan's Travels, The Palm Beach Story, The Great Moment*), in Hitchcock's *Foreign Correspondent* and in George Stevens's *The More the Merrier,* he is a revelation. During this important phase of his career, Frances was winding down hers, although in 1943 she starred in one of the classics of low-budget suspense, *I Walked with a Zombie.* Joel's shrewd business mind and real estate investments (his friend Will Rogers advised the young actor to buy land and go into ranching, and even helped him select his first property) have made the McCreas one of the richest couples in California. But Frances still calls him "Pop" and cooks dinner nearly every night at their Camarillo ranch. There have been a few rough patches in the marriage over the years, but every fall the McCreas try to go back to Stony Brook, Long Island, to relive their honeymoon. The simple life agrees with them, and Frances, now in her mid-70s but still size 6, could pass for an ingenue any day if not for her stunning silver hair.

GRETA NISSEN

Three hours north of Los Angeles and more than 2,000 feet above the Pacific coastline, the Santa Ynez Mountains are alive with the sound of show biz. John Travolta poured his profits from *Saturday Night Fever* and *Grease* into a ranch there, and back in 1974 Ronald and Nancy Reagan plunked down half a million for a 688-acre spread, Rancho del Cielo, above the Travolta property. Looking down on all this from her 1,400-acre retreat is one of the more elusive ex-stars of stage and screen, Greta Nissen. Long before Liv Ullmann, Greta was the first Norwegian import in the 1920s when Hollywood was overflowing with exotic sirens flushed out of Europe. Winding up the mountain road, visitors come to a locked gate with eight padlocks for each of the adjoining properties. Stuart Eckert, Greta's millionaire husband for over 40 years, says the President's lock combination, 1980, was a good omen for his election. Eckert is not happy about "Ronnie baby's" security forces who now invade their private domain. He is also less than enchanted with talk about his wife's career. She could never be accused of "wallowing in the past," he states firmly. Tiny and reticent, Greta herself is just as blasé. "I'm so happy with my life with Stuart. We met on a blind date and I don't know if he even knew who I once was," she confides, quite pleased about that possibility. "I get an occasional birthday card from a fan—they must be pretty old! Somewhere in the cellar, I've got old photos, things like that, but who cares?" Nothing in the Scandinavian sim-

plicity of the ranch house acknowledges former stardom. Eckert watches his wife gamely climb over the porch railing for Horst, then suggests she put on his cowboy boots "to look like a cowgal." She willingly pulls on the boots, four or five sizes too big. "They always told me what to do in the movies too."

Born in Oslo in 1906, Greta was an angelic child who became the protégée of the Queen of Norway. At six she was placed at the Royal Opera House school in Copenhagen. Her father was killed in World War I, and she and her mother, a costume designer, traveled throughout Europe, Greta performing in ballet and mime. She made a sensational Broadway debut in a pantomime interlude called *A Kiss in Xanadu* in the Kaufman-Connelly comedy *Beggar on Horseback*. Hollywood called and the critics tossed adjectives such as "beguiling" and "sparkling" at the new find, but her movies (*Lost—A Wife, The Lady of the Harem, The Popular Sin*) were anything but. Greta, if known at all today, is remembered for the part she lost. Howard Hughes cast her in *Hell's Angels*, but with the advent of sound he reshot it as a talkie sans Greta. Replacement Jean Harlow became a star overnight. Greta's English actually was—and is—quite intelligible, and in a dozen sound films and later on the stage, mainly in England, where she moved after the annulment of her first marriage, Greta proved it. The sun is high over the Pacific horizon but the horseflies are out in full force. Stuart puts his arm around his wife. "That's enough pictures," he says, leading her back into the house. "Greta may have been a famous actress once upon a time, but to me she's just my old chum."

GINGER ROGERS

The March 19, 1926, issue of *The Vaudeville News,* price 10 cents, introduced a new face to show business. Beaming broadly on the cover was a bobbed-haired 14-year-old with chipmunk cheeks. The caption announced: "Ginger Rogers, Champion Charleston Dancer of Texas, Now Playing Western Vaudeville." Fifty-eight years later almost to the day, March 9, 1984, to be exact, Horst visited Ginger's Rancho Mirage home to take this picture. Unlike the Charleston, vaudeville and bobbed hair, Ginger's still going strong. "And howdy," she says, explaining that she's been out of action as a performer lately only because she is so hard at work on her autobiography. "Money, marbles and chalk, people are going to say, Does Ginger bite? No, Ginger snaps! " Two months later in Washington, D.C., at the American Film Institute's gala in her honor, where she presented the Smithsonian with the chiffon gown she wore when she danced the Piccolino with Fred Astaire in *Top Hat,* Ginger put it on the line: "This must make me an institution." Then she winked, "That the gown survived, not only the years but the filming itself, is a miracle." It's no miracle, however, that Ginger has. No performer has ever worked harder, no actress thought she could accomplish as much ("Well, Shakespeare I didn't do"), no star ever gave more to a career, losing five husbands along the way and becoming the highest paid movie star in 1945. Today the Astaire-Rogers musicals are among the sublime treasures of our film heritage, but most people don't realize that when the series ended in 1939, it was Ginger who was riding high as RKO's top star while Fred had been named box office poison by the theater exhibitors. Years later, Ginger would have a word for their relationship. "I think the experience with Fred was a divine blessing. It blessed me, I know, and I don't think blessings are one-sided." She also would joke, "My first picture was *Kitty Foyle* (her Oscar win in 1940). It was my mother who made all those pictures with Fred." She rarely joked about Mom, nor did Fred about his mother. Both had case histories that define the term stage mother; in fact, their mothers lived with them until their deaths.

Lela Owens McMath Rogers was a re-

markable and ambitious woman. Her first child died in infancy and her third was stillborn. When she left her first husband, he kidnapped little Ginger, not once but twice. The child was sent to her grandparents in Kansas City while Lela went off to Hollywood to peddle scripts. During World War I, Lela did publicity for the Marine Corps and became the superpatriot who would support the blacklist 30 years later. She made certain that Ginger had the best, including piano and dance lessons. In 1925, when Eddie Foy was playing Fort Worth, where Lela and Ginger then lived with Lela's second husband, Ginger filled in for an ailing chorine. Within months she was on the Texas-Oklahoma circuit as Ginger and Her Redheads. Lela managed the act and wrote lots of the special material, particularly the silly baby talk that to this day Ginger lapses into as if she is still just a kid at heart. She made good use of this facility in the hilarious pig-Latin verse of "We're in the Money" ("Er-way In-ay E-thay Oney-may") she sang in *Gold Diggers of 1933* and then in one of her brightest comedies, *The Major and the Minor* in 1942, when she captured the essence of a sarcastic brat with her little girl voice. Though Ginger's movie career ended with *Oh, Men! Oh, Women!* in 1957 (she did a few cheapies in the 1960s), she continued to entertain in clubs around the world and in the theater—*Hello, Dolly!* on Broadway and *Mame* in London. She took on some sidelines too—designing a line of lingerie for JC Penney. And of course her films with and without Fred are everywhere.

Talking with her several years ago at the Waldorf-Astoria in New York, she philosophized firmly: "Longevity is not the point. I just like being part of the fabric, or maybe I should say I like the traffic, I'll never put my hands in my lap." If the traffic has thinned during the last decade, she has never let it come to a complete halt. "I see work as harvest time, the joyous time. And my religious background helps me maintain my equilibrium." Ginger is a Christian Scientist, hence she has never had a face-lift. "Age, I don't speak of it," she says. "If people have to have a sense of limitation on their thinking, it's their problem, not mine. I do have a birth date, so does everyone, but if you're constantly talking about it, well, it's like the old saying, 'It's the head that thinks it, it's the head that hurts.' The best date I know is 1492—I don't know any others."

Ginger also hates to discuss her private life and offers "No comment" on the romance with Howard Hughes. Hughes's late confidant, Noel Dietrich, revealed that Ginger was the only woman who ever made Hughes cry, and Terry Moore states that Katharine Hepburn was terribly jealous when Hughes took a liking to Ginger. Ginger will go as far as to admit, "I've made lots of mistakes. I take credit for them just as I take credit for my successes. I've been earning a living since my Sunday school days and I think I've been inspired to do what I've done. People make choices, but cynics make the wrong ones, then they keep stumbling. I try to turn my mistakes into stepping stones to the right road. I believe life understood is like mathematics understood—better." Garson Kanin, who directed Ginger in *Bachelor Mother* and *Tom, Dick and Harry,* wasn't thinking of religious or philosophic considerations, just a wonderfully vital and attractive all-American entertainer, when he wrote: "Ginger is a genuine movie star, and therefore a permanent presence. A movie star is a creation that, like a painting or a statue or a symphony, does not age."

VIRGINIA BRUCE

She's changed her mind, she wants to be photographed, even in the hospital. She's going to wear her good pearls." Virginia Bruce's sister-in-law is on the phone, explaining how much this might mean to the actress who 40 years earlier was called "The Most Beautiful Blonde in the Movies"—quite a claim in the era of Marlene Dietrich, Madeleine Carroll and Carole Lombard. The hospital room is small and spare, a sole bouquet is on the side table. The note in the flowers reads: "It was wonderful seeing one of my all-time loves. Bob Hope." A golden girl in MGM's golden era, Virginia decorated the top of the gigantic wedding-cake column in the lavish "A Pretty Girl Is Like a Melody" production number in *The Great Ziegfeld*. Bedecked in sequins and feathers, she led a parade of showgirls in "You Never Looked So Beautiful Before" in that famous movie biography. Now she is propped up in a metal chair. Her voice, smoky and seductive, alone defies the years. "I can't smile for the camera, really I can't. I'll look serious for you, I'm *so* dramatic anyway." Then she whispers with a touch of heartbreak in her voice: "Do you know Norma Shearer is just down the hall? She was the biggest of them all, and here she is blind and dying, after all that, all that fame and riches and now this. Maybe I haven't had it so tough. Two of my husbands died on me and my daughter's been on welfare, but I've got eight grandchildren and well . . ." Virginia tries to smile but settles for lighting up a Chesterfield. "People do remember me (her last work was in 1960 as Kim Novak's mother in *Strangers When We Meet*) and God, I just signed 15 old stills for somebody, things I never had ever seen before. I've been in and out of this place (The Motion Picture Country House and Hospital) so much people just know where to find me."

Born in Minneapolis, Virginia was touring a Hollywood studio when a director spotted the teenager. She learned on the job along with other blonde beginners like Jean Harlow. Though no Harlow, she did marry the silent screen's great lover, John Gilbert, but it didn't help the career of either. In the mid-1930s, she was a workhorse at MGM in second leads. Aside from the spoiled showgirl in *The Great Ziegfeld*, her most memorable moment came in *Born to Dance*, when she introduced Cole Porter's "I've Got You Under My Skin." A third marriage, to a younger man, a Turk, in the 1940s more or less ended her career but not the headlines. Her husband was in one controversy after another and ended up serving 19 months in a Turkish prison, charged with fraudulent business dealings. Virginia tried to get help through the State Department. They finally divorced in 1964. Shortly after our photo session, Virginia Bruce died at the age of 72. The obituaries all observed the passing of "one of the celebrated beauties of the screen" and listed her leading men—James Cagney, James Stewart, Fredric March, William Powell, Robert Taylor. But that late afternoon in her hospital room when she finally managed a faint, touching smile, Virginia wondered aloud, "Do you think when I'm gone, anyone will remember that I had awfully dreamy eyes?"

MAUREEN O'SULLIVAN

High up over Manhattan's Central Park, Maureen O'Sullivan steps over her grandchildren's toys and moves to the window. As she glances back over her shoulder, Maureen's big, beautiful blue eyes catch the light and sparkle. The same twinkle attracted film director Frank Borzage to a teenage colleen he met in Dublin in 1930. County Roscommon's gift to Hollywood has survived the long haul, but then her father, Colonel Charles O'Sullivan of the Connaught Rangers, always said he never had to worry about the convent-educated Maureen. "Strong-willed and downright sturdy" is how he described his dainty daughter. At 19 she arrived in the land of dreams with her mother to make a winsome debut in John McCormick's *Song O' My Heart.* Her milky complexion photographed like porcelain and her Irish lilt was a welcome sound. Fox almost groomed her to succeed Janet Gaynor, then America's Sweetheart and on suspension. But once Gaynor settled her money demands, Maureen became just another starlet on the loose. For the rest of her life, personally and professionally, she needed all the inner strength her father boasted about. Maureen free-lanced, then settled at MGM, a resident ingenue. To her credit, she wasn't ground into the scenery in support of MGM's scene-stealers—Marie Dressler and Wallace Beery in *Tugboat Annie,* Norma Shearer in *The Barretts of Wimpole Street,* Garbo in *Anna Karenina,* the Marx Brothers in *A Day at the Races.* Though it made her a household favorite, her "me, Jane" role in the six MGM Tarzan films pitted Maureen against man (non-actor Johnny Weissmuller) and beast (the chimps bit and mauled her). The third in the series introduced her to a macho Australian writer-director, John Farrow, whom she married in 1936. When he joined the Canadian Royal Navy, Maureen moved to Canada—none too soon, for she was fast becoming Hollywood's oldest ingenue. She didn't act from 1942 to 1948 but had the big family she always wanted and nursed Farrow back to health when he was wounded in action. Tragedy struck when their oldest, Michael, was killed in a plane-training accident, and again when Maria de Lourdes, who would become Mia Farrow, was stricken with polio. In 1963 Maureen lost her husband and she returned to a full-time career. Thanks to Mia, Maureen was briefly Frank Sinatra's mother-in-law. She herself found love again with actor Robert Ryan, but he died of cancer before they could marry. To her friends, the widow Farrow became known as Mother Courage. Working mostly on the stage, Maureen opened to acclaim on Broadway in 1980 in the all-star revival of Paul Osborn's *Morning's at Seven.* In the summer of 1983, Maureen married a New York State businessman. With her eyes clear and shining, she turns from the park view and smiles: "I'm ready for anything. And it'll be time for great-grandchildren before I know it."

VIRGINIA CHERRILL

A t the end of City Lights, *the blind girl who has regained her sight, thanks to the Tramp [Chaplin], sees him for the first time. She has imagined and anticipated him as princely . . . and it has never seriously occurred to him that he is inadequate. . . . and he recognizes himself for the first time, through the terrible changes in her face. The camera just exchanges a few quiet close-ups of the emotions which shift and intensify in each face. It is enough to shrivel the heart to see, and it is the greatest piece of acting and the highest moment in movies.*"—James Agee in *Comedy's Greatest Era*

Though she went on to make a few other films, become the first Mrs. Cary Grant and later the ninth Countess of Jersey, Virginia Cherrill's moment of immortality is as the blind girl in the Chaplin masterpiece. More than 50 years later, standing in the living room of her Santa Barbara home, her Jack Russell terrier, Daisy, an armful, she reluctantly looks back. "I have never been able to say much good about Chaplin, so I haven't said much period," she confesses. "He was hard on me (it was her first acting job), and I was his prisoner for two years. (It was in production 534 days, and at one point Chaplin fired her, only to rehire her.) He was always out playing tennis, while I was never allowed to leave the studio. Then, too, I always felt he was disloyal, first to England and then to America. Now when I see *City Lights* all I can think of is what a friend of mine said: 'It looks as if your hair was put on with a biscuit cutter!' "

A peerless beauty who was also brainy, also rich, Virginia lived up to her Cinderella girl reputation on both sides of the Atlantic. "Those days were fun, but girls were really treated terribly. I used to go sailing on weekends with rich guys like Milton Bren (later married to Claire Trevor) and lovely young things like Polly Ann Young and Sally Blane (Loretta Young's older sisters), and we girls were *allowed* to polish the boat brass." Yet every artist of the day came calling. "I was photographed to death by Steichen, Beaton, Diana Wilding," she says, standing in front of a 1938 portrait by Sorine. Gesturing at it, she adds, "That character had me do 33 sittings because he painted with about three hairs in his brush." Today she's a homebody. "I learned to cook after 50." Stopping in Santa Barbara in 1951, she ended up staying and buying a house, while her husband, Florian Martini, went on to establish a reputation there with Lockheed as an engineer and scientist. "Florian is a Pole born in Russia with an Italian great-grandfather. During those horrible war days in London, I worked with the Red Cross. I met about 13,000 Polish pilots in the RAF—and, well, he was the last one I met, but when he flew in, I flew out. We've been married since 1948, and now he's a real Polish cowboy here in California." She says she remains on good terms with Cary Grant. "Cary was married to his career. That's something that could never have been said of me."

CARMEL MYERS

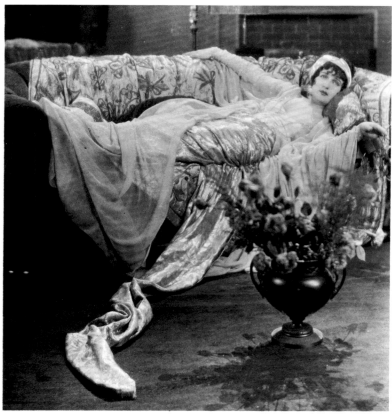

The day before she died at age 80 in the fall of 1980, just two weeks after this photograph was taken, Carmel Myers was busy pushing her new perfume, named Carmel of course, at classy I. Magnin in Beverly Hills. All blonde curls, flowing gestures and infectious smiles, Carmel made a strong impression as a pitchwoman. No longer a household name despite the fact that she was always pushing something, usually herself, she was an extrovert to the end, which came fast and unexpectedly. In the 1930s, after her screen acting had faded away and she was busy rearing a family with her second husband, big-time lawyer-agent Ralph Blum, she moved into Gloria Swanson's estate and opened it up for many a fancy party. She always had a good time at her own festivities, while making sure those around her had the same. Carmel's guest book became her Oscar, filled as it was with cheery notes from the likes of Harpo Marx ("Here I am again") and Somerset Maugham ("Thanking you for a lovely party"). After one shindig, F. Scott Fitzgerald felt moved to write this verse he entitled "After Reading Through An Autograph Album":

Carmel and Ralph—you grand guys
Paid plenty soup for these sweet lies,
Poured plenty gin to make this
*   collection*
Cut plenty cake to win this "Affec-
*   tion."*
Lots of these "Darlings," lots of these
*   "Dears"*
Foamed from the tops of costly
*   beers. . . .*
Minds clearly vacant, thoughts quite
*   alarming—*

Charming, CHARMING, OH SO
*   CHARMING!*
Watch them—see their elbows bend,
Fill 'em up again, and they call you
*   FRIEND.*
There's just one who is real sincere:
That's the man who is writing here
Thinks you're a likely lad and lass
(Hey, gal, please fill up that glass!).

Carmel's career got a firm foothold when her father, a rabbi and one of the founders of Temple Sinai in Los Angeles, became an unofficial adviser to D. W. Griffith for his masterwork, *Intolerance*, in 1916. Both a screen test and screen success followed, and by the end of the silent era Carmel had chalked up over 50 movie credits, counting as co-stars the matinee idols of the era—Ru-dolph Valentino, John Gilbert and John Barrymore. Her only consistently revived silent is *Ben-Hur*, but she is barely recognizable in platinum tresses and Erte headgear playing the Egyptian seductress Iras. Never quite retiring (she dabbled in radio and early television), Carmel, widowed a second time, descended on Hollywood again after more than 20 years in New York City, where she headed up the cosmetic enterprise Zizanie. These last years were jolly, and whether on talk shows reliving parties at Pickfair or dropping names of the great designers who decked her out, Carmel relished being a nostalgia party girl. In 1977 she even showed up for a bit in *Won Ton Ton, the Dog That Saved Hollywood*. Life, she said, was as sweet as the Carmel perfume that permeated her apartment. Never less than fun-loving, she claimed, "I always said I'd rather play vamps. Nice ladies are just like wallpaper."

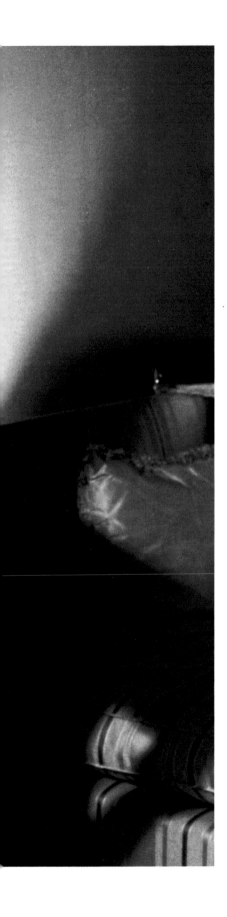

JOAN FONTAINE

Cary Grant to Joan Fontaine in Alfred Hitchcock's *Suspicion:* "Hello, monkey face."

Joan Fontaine, now in her 60s, would be a vision of well-preserved blonde beauty even without plastic surgery. She has taken good care of herself, and she says she had to do it all herself because nobody else has ever come into her life to do it for her. After four marriages, she concludes that "men don't want wives, they want mothers." Looking good is the one thing Joan holds onto from her days of stardom. She still has a hang-up about her face when it comes to being photographed. In the middle of the living room in her large Manhattan co-op, Joan had Horst climb an old battered ladder to get the shot and the side of her face she wants on view. She likes to be photographed from overhead, left side, her cheeks hollowed out by shadows—the old Dietrich trick. The Fontaine jaw always had a masculine squareness but Joan's good cheekbones disguise the fact. Her countenance is slightly asymmetrical and her right eyelid tends to droop toward the upturned right corner of her mouth. Playing her bitchier roles (*Ivy, Serenade*), she would raise her chin and the most arresting sexual sneer would come into play. That look was a killer, coming as it did later in her career, after she had portrayed so many child-women—shy, repressed young things in *The Women, Rebecca, The Constant Nymph.*

Nowadays Joan is mostly smiles, but not because she has had many good acting offers lately or because she wrought revenge on older sister Olivia de Havilland in her slight but acrimonious autobiography, *No Bed of Roses.* She has had to put forth the friendly front on television as pitchwoman for romantic pulp (the Silhouette series) or in guest appearances in shopping centers for Hummel ware. Joan is as much a perfectionist with these chores as with her acting—"If movies taught me anything, it was discipline." One television commercial, she confesses, had to be reshot 50 times before she was satisfied. She is blunt with her self-assessment: "I've held up well. My hands are bad, but I always had bad hands. I don't think many people *really* know me anymore. They just can't place my face." But Joan won't look back. "I never see my movies. I never looked at them when I made them. I did see *The Constant Nymph* not too long ago since it's been out of circulation. When it was over I said, 'Get me to the nearest bar and give me a double vodka.' " That film is a gem, and Joan as the sickly teenager whose heart literally breaks for the love of a composer, played by that old breaker of hearts Charles Boyer, gives one of her most fervent performances. Her Hitchcock work, in constant revival, also stands the test of time; few actresses are so identified with a single movie (perhaps Greer Garson as Mrs. Miniver) as Joan with *Rebecca*. She won the Oscar the following year, 1941, for another mousy wife in *Suspicion* but it was an instance where the award was really compensation for the previous performance. Lesser known but widely admired in critical circles is the period romance *Letter from an Unknown Woman,* directed by Max Ophuls, which her own company produced. Again Joan played a teenager moving with ease into adulthood and again fatally drawn to a musician, Louis Jourdan. This masterpiece turns up on many "best films of all time" lists and is probably Joan's crowning glory. That was 1948.

After so many years, she is ripe for a genuine comeback. But whether or not she will have a chance to bloom again as an actress is questionable. Several years ago she did *The Lion in Winter* in an English-language stage version in Vienna with enthusiastic response. When she tried to set up a U.S. tour, she had to face the hard news that the author preferred a "name" like Glenda Jackson. It is impossible to judge the toll such disappointments take when you have your beauty, your talent, yet the years are running out. "But I've always been interested in so many other things besides acting," Joan says with a shrug. "My fourth time on a golf course I shot a hole in one (her last husband was an editor at *Sports Illustrated*). I was flying solo after just a few lessons. I have my interior decorating license too. I just love to travel—I've been marooned in Kashmir! And I've done well with my money (though for years she made little under personal contract to David O. Selznick, while he cleaned up loaning her out—she received only $12,000 for *Rebecca*)."

Joan doesn't dwell on some things—her daughters, for example. Daughter Deborah was born in 1948 and reared by her father, producer William

Dozier, Joan's second husband, after an ugly six-year custody fight; and Joan adopted a Peruvian girl on a South American trip in the early 1950s. The saddest chapter in her autobiography details how Olivia mistreated her at the time of their mother's death. The only family picture in Joan's apartment is of her father, who married his Japanese housekeeper after their mother left him—Joan was born in Tokyo in 1917 and became a naturalized U.S. citizen in 1943. Other photos are of friends—Eleanor Roosevelt, Ralph Bunche, Daphne du Maurier, and Adlai Stevenson, with whom she was so in love. "I always wanted to mingle with older people," Joan says. "I wanted to learn from them. You see I don't believe that when you lose your youth, you lose everything."

OLIVIA DE HAVILLAND

Errol Flynn, Leslie Howard, James Stewart and Howard Hughes fell in love with her. Ernie Pyle, seeing her on a World War II tour in the South Pacific, wrote: "Her face is so beautiful, all I could do was stand and stare." Olivia de Havilland was Hollywood's "blue-ribbon bachelor girl," the definitive Maid Marian to Flynn's Robin Hood, the ideal actress to imbue a heart-wrenching dimension to the insipid Melanie Wilkes in *Gone with the Wind.* But this "lady of rapturous loveliness" was an independent type. Just as she had walked out of her mother's home at 16 because she couldn't get on with stepfather George Fontaine, whose name her sister Joan would use, she took on Warner Bros. in the test case that broke the hold of the studios over their contract players. Unemployed for almost two years, she jeopardized her career but, as Bette Davis once said, "fought like a tigress to free actors of perpetual bondage." A victrix, she should have been a Queen Bee of Hollywood and almost was with the roles that followed: *To Each His Own* (her first Oscar), *The Dark Mirror, The Snake Pit* and *The Heiress* (her second Oscar). But Olivia made bad choices. When she finally married at age 30 in 1946, she picked novelist Marcus Goodrich, by whom she had a son. Joan said what everyone was thinking at the time: "All I know about Goodrich is that he's had four wives and written one book; too bad it's not the other way around." Olivia turned down the film of *A Streetcar Named Desire* and tackled the stage—her Juliet was too old, her Candida too young. In 1955 she moved to Paris to be with second husband *Paris Match* editor Pierre Galante. She bore him a daughter but they soon went separate ways. For years Olivia has lived on the prestige she won in the 1940s. Her recent work has been nontaxing television—the killer in Agatha Christie's *Murder Is Easy* and the Queen Mom in *Charles and Diana: A Royal Romance,* in which Olivia looked just like her own mother, Lilian Fontaine. Nowadays Olivia talks about leaving her 10-bedroom Paris town house and moving back to the States. If she ever finishes her autobiography, the old De Havilland fighting spirit may yet set off sparks when she airs her side of the sibling rivalry with Joan.

ESTHER RALSTON

July 10, 1979. "Photographed by James Wong Howe, in *Peter Pan*, Esther was so beautiful (!) in the whole world not a single mirror on the wall could have said 'No' to her. That beauty alone makes her worthy of remembrance in your *Life* piece. Love, Louise."

Two years after Louise Brooks's suggestion—she and Esther Ralston met in the 1920s at Paramount—Horst and I drove up to a mobile home near Ventura, California. On the porch of the trailer, waiting with open arms as if she had known us as long as she had Louise, was the effervescent Esther. A lemon pie hot out of the oven was waiting, too, and enough tales to rival Louise's *Lulu in Hollywood*. It was easy to understand why everybody loved her. How sad then that more people cannot see her work, that so little is preserved; even her finest hour, in Josef von Sternberg's 1929 *The Case of Lena Smith,* is lost (she played a peasant girl who becomes a servant in her lover's house). Film historians can only

speculate that Sternberg's wizardry was as spellbinding with Esther as it was with Marlene Dietrich.

Esther serves the pie and starts to gab. "Where do I begin?" Though she has come through a cancer operation, had three failed marriages and never reached the top ring of stardom, she is brimming with enthusiasm. "I've been working on a book, and now maybe since I came out here to retire—well, a TV commercial doesn't count, does it— maybe I'll get it done." In 1904 at age two, Esther made her debut at the Magnificent Milk Fund Benefit in Bar Harbor, Maine, where she had been born to a physical culture director who soon had his family touring vaudeville. Esther hands me a Xerox of an old theatrical flier. "The Ralston Family, Metropolitan Entertainers—With Baby Esther, 'America's Greatest Juliet.' " "Oh, I was playing Shakespeare at six. It was easy for me, my brothers are the ones who had trouble, they had to double in the girls' roles." She made her film debut appropriately as an angel in Clara Kimball Young's *The Deep Purple,* filmed in New Jersey "around 1914."

Esther's father moved the family troupe west because of the infantile paralysis scare. She became an extra and found work with Chaplin in *The Kid* ("When he lost his inspiration, he would just go and play beautiful classical melodies on the organ while Jackie Coogan and I had fun in the swimming pool"), Lon Chaney (*Oliver Twist,* again with Coogan) and Tom Mix ("He had a car about a block and a half long, and when you opened the door a sign lit up with his name—he died in a car crash, you know"). She can tell you how Gary Cooper got started (and fired once) and how Clara Bow was every bit as wild as her reputation "but so much fun. We got on, though she preferred the company of men—and I do mean men."

When sound arrived, Esther made the transition, and for a time "The American Venus"—the tag had stuck since her 1925 film of that title—seemed destined for major stardom. Then Paramount dropped her, and when MGM showed interest, "I was pregnant with my daughter Mary. We called her the $100,000 baby because that's what I lost." After working in England, she did make a deal with MGM, but they loaned her out to other studios (rumor said it was because Louis B. Mayer liked "blonde *ladies*" but Esther didn't like the big boss). Her only MGM film was Joan Crawford's *Sadie McKee* in 1934, in which she stole Gene Raymond from the star. "That was all right with Joan, but she didn't like the way I did my eye makeup—same as hers." After two more marriages and two more children, her film work ended in 1941; then came radio, stock and television. By 1956, she was head of the boys' department at a B. Altman's on Long Island. Esther hung in. In the 1960s she did a soap opera and became a talent agent. Before moving to California, she worked 10 years at an electrical supply store in Glens Falls, New York. "In 1975, while still selling my lighting fixtures, I got to do *Arsenic and Old Lace* in Lake George, coming full circle from Baby Juliet in that part of the country 70 years earlier."

The lemon pie is about gone, and a 70ish nature boy in shorts has stopped by. Obviously Esther is the life of her new community. "Since I was never a drunk or a dope fiend or went around having affairs, I shall just have to write the facts and the funny side," she says. "I'm calling it 'Some Day We'll Laugh.' "

POLA NEGRI

Deep in the heart of Texas, down San Antonio way, far from the scenes of her grand passions on two continents, resides the last of the great movie sirens. Bejeweled and besequined, Pola Negri epitomizes all that is larger than life about our cinematic icons. She won't speak her age—most record books list December 31, 1894, in Yanowa, Poland, and 1914 as her first film appearance. But she does allow that Rudolph Valentino was her one true love ("We only had one year together") and that Gloria Swanson, Marlene Dietrich and all the rest of the femme fatales just followed her pioneering style. Indeed, she was the first international star, arriving in Hollywood from Berlin, where she had been the reigning light of UFA under the great director Ernst Lubitsch. World-weary yet hot-blooded, her personality in steamy if now ludicrous melodramas helped throw off the yoke of Victorian propriety for young women in the 1920s. Despite the outer trappings—she claims to have been the first to make boots and turbans fashionable—Pola could be an earthy comedienne too. Her rivalry with Swanson at Paramount was mostly studio hype, but she did beat Gloria in the race for titles—Pola bagged both a count and a prince as husbands while Gloria never got above a marquis. When Valentino died in 1926, Pola was part of the headlines. She raced across the continent by train, stopping only long enough to buy $3,000 worth of mourning garb and to order an 11-by-6-foot pall of 4,000 scarlet roses for the casket. The public ate it up, but her affairs didn't guarantee patronization of her increasingly dated movies. By the end of the silents she was finished.

Pola returned to Europe, eventually making six

films back at UFA, then under Goebbels's control. Rumors circulated that he hated her, questioning her bloodline (she is a devout Catholic today). But Hitler liked an American star in his firmament (Dietrich refused to make films there in the 1930s). Pola stayed in Europe a little too long and, though she worked for the Red Cross after war broke out, had trouble getting on one of the last boats out of Lisbon in 1941. She was broke and needed to work, but a feeble 1943 comedy, *Hi Diddle Diddle,* did nothing for her. Several years later she met Margaret West and money cares were to end forever. A colorful Texas millionairess and "patron of the arts," she befriended Pola and their years together were happy-go-lucky.

Surrounded by old masters inherited from her late patroness, Pola slowly moves across the living room of her stately condo. Nearly blind ("It was the lights in those early days, they burned out our eyes") and having endured many operations to help save some sight, she plays a recording of "Paradise," the song she made famous in her first talkie, *A Woman Commands*. She hums along. She speaks of Lady Bird Johnson wanting her art collection for a museum and shows off an incredible solid gold vanity set—"My parting gift from UFA 60 years ago." She has donated her films to the local university, St. Mary's, but she is proudest of a simple plaque from the West German government. "To Pola Negri, For her long and extraordinary achievement in the development of German film." It is the only such honor ever bestowed by that country on a movie star, she says. Once, when asked if she would change anything in her fabulous life, Pola played the answer to the hilt in authentic Negri-ese: "I would relinquish neither inner scars nor external glories. I have wept and laughed, been foolish and wise. There is an edge of triumph in the peacefulness of my old age."

ALEXIS SMITH

Second acts don't usually play as well as Alexis Smith's. She started mighty young but usually played older—"That's why people think I'm ancient." First as a leggy Warner Bros. starlet, then as an aloof second lead—"I was a co-star with the emphasis on the co"—she ended up a frosty leading lady. "That wasn't so much fun," she notes. "One big star was so short that I never got to wear shoes. Let's call him Char-

lie. Whenever he got temperamental, I'd just yell, 'Get the apple box for Charlie.' "

Alexis was born in British Columbia in 1921, but her father moved the family to California for her mother's health. Reared strict Scotch Presbyterian, she wore homemade clothes and was never allowed to date like her Hollywood High schoolmates Lana Turner, Nanette Fabray and Bonita Granville. At 16, she won a declamation contest, but when the talent scouts came calling, her dad refused their offers. "I loved him for doing that," she says today, adding, "most child actresses just don't last very long or have happy lives." When she turned 19, her father gave in. Alexis's studio years were good experience, but she admits, "I had too much respect for authority and never spoke up. I did grow up fast, anyone would being in the dressing room next to Bette Davis and hearing her early morning phone calls with her mother! I was a utility girl, really. If Davis or Ida Lupino or Ann Sheridan turned down something, then it fell on me, and nobody is that versatile." She thinks that she was probably just overwhelmed by "being in pictures. Worse, I was too tall in an era that adored cute little Betty Grable." So Alexis saw her movie days peter out in a dozen years and she turned to stock and touring Broadway shows, quite content that her husband, Craig Stevens, was becoming a household name in the 1960s as Peter Gunn.

Then, in 1971, Hal Prince and Michael Bennett brought Alexis to Broadway in Stephen Sondheim's legendary *Follies*. Finally she had a second act to prove the sweetness of late-blooming success. She won the Tony as best musical actress and found herself on the cover of *Time*. While *Follies* was about how time erodes marriage, wastes beauty and twists careers, Alexis ironically suffered no such fate. Her marriage was (and is) steadfast, her beauty never more breathtaking, and the career swung back into orbit never to descend again. Now as the stylish villainess in *Dallas*, she is as statuesque and sharp-tongued as ever. One night in a restaurant, a light bulb clicks on inside our waiter's head. He recognizes Alexis and approaches with a wide grin. "I've seen you on the late show." She snaps, "You've been staying up too late." She's one stunner of an ex–movie star who doesn't have to look back.

OLIVE
CAREY

Olive Golden Carey, who is somewhere in her 90s, is the last link to the rugged pioneer days of the early westerns. Swaying in her rocker, she is Whistler's Mother gone country. "I've rented this place for 25 years," she says about her ranch outside of Santa Barbara. "The 33 acres were originally part of an old Spanish land grant." The record books don't list much about her acting career, but as the wife of Harry Carey she was witness to the birth of the movies. Harry was born in the Bronx and studied law, but he turned out to be the most natural of western stars, the opposite of the stoic William S. Hart. With his friend John Ford, another easterner in love with the vanishing West, Harry made a series of cowboy two-reelers and features for Universal between 1917 and 1921. After *Trader Horn*, MGM's ill-fated 1931 African epic, he slid into supporting roles. Olive and Harry married in 1913 after he had already been launched at Biograph under D. W. Griffith. Since he never learned to drive, Olive took him to the set every morning and then returned to take him home at night. It was only a matter of time and she was in front of the camera too. "It was nothing but making all 12 faces," she shrugs today, taking a puff on her cigarette. "The only good thing about the movies was the money. I got $5 a day with a four-day-a-week guarantee." When Harry died in 1947, Ford dedicated the remake of Carey's silent, *Three Godfathers*, to him—"Bright Star of the Early Western Sky." In that film Ford helped to kick off the screen career of Harry Carey, Jr., who co-starred with John Wayne. Carey Jr. eased into the Ford stock company but never attained the popularity of his dad. Olive's swan song was *The Searchers*, a "tragedy of a loner" as Ford himself described this 1956 landmark epic."It was my last, all right," says Olive, "but it was Duke's (John Wayne's) greatest." The walls of her ranch house form a rogue's gallery of western icons. One autographed photo stands out. "To Olive, Best wishes and everything that goes with the sage. Tom Mix."

CLAUDETTE COLBERT

A sunny September afternoon on Fifth Avenue in 1980. "I'll be 77 on Saturday and Frank (Sinatra) is tossing a party in London. Then I'm going down, or is it up, the Nile with the Annenbergs, and I hope to have an audience with the Pope on the way back." Claudette Colbert has just made a spectacular entrance into the grand living room of her friend Robert Ellsworth, the Oriental antique authority, with whom she often stayed until she got her own New York pied-à-terre. She fluffs up her black satin ball gown. "Oh, it's nothing, last

year's Nina Ricci," she says, pointing a touch of toe from under the rich fabric. The famous legs come into view and it is impossible to believe that 55 years have passed since Walter Winchell first called her "Legs Colbert" and almost five decades since Claudette proved "the limb mightier than the thumb" in the memorable hitchhiking scene from *It Happened One Night.* She chats briefly with Horst about their minor vices, namely smoking. But within moments come the infamous Colbert dictates as she arranges herself for the portrait. "I only have one side, really I do. I have a terrible nose. My key light was always overhead. It straightened my nose." When she was the biggest female star at Paramount in the late 1930s and early 1940s, the sets were built around her good side so only the left profile would be photographed. She admits, "When it comes to details, I'm a horror," which once prompted Noel Coward to complain: "If Claudette only had a neck, I'd wring it." She still curls, cuts, washes and bleaches her own hair. "I've always done it and I know just what to do. I have a gray streak right down the middle and lots on the side, but it's all mixed and looks bad. My friends tell me to keep dyeing it for a few more years." Candid but captivating, glamorous yet real, Claudette is the envy of all the stars of her generation. She has never lost her looks—the famous short haircut with bangs and those round apple cheeks lineless to this day. Her sophisticated insouciance and effortless charm have never run dry.

Claudette was born in Paris in 1903, her father a banker "who suffered reverses" and brought the family to New York. He later became her agent. During the 1920s she left behind her interests in painting and millinery for the lucrative world of the stage. She had to make

nearly two dozen unworthy movies before her own saucy identity shone through. But there were early signs, particularly when she and Miriam Hopkins sang "Jazz Up Your Lingerie" for Ernst Lubitsch in *The Smiling Lieutenant.* She worked for Cecil B. DeMille in *Four Frightened People, Cleopatra* and *The Sign of the Cross.* In the latter, he floated her in "$10,000 worth of Grade A asses' milk" for one of the campiest bathtub scenes ever. But it was Frank

Capra on poverty row at Columbia who turned around her career with *It Happened One Night* (she and Clark Gable both won Oscars), and for the next decade she ranked with Carole Lombard, Irene Dunne and Jean Arthur as the greatest comediennes in Hollywood. But Claudette also sublimated her gaiety for drama and was the mother to end all mothers in David O. Selznick's World War II soap opera, *Since You Went Away.* In 1950, two weeks before starting *All About Eve,* she broke her back and Bette Davis inherited Margo Channing, a role sorely needed to rejuvenate Colbert's sliding star. In the early 1950s she went

off to Europe to save taxes, and when she replaced Margaret Sullavan on Broadway in *Janus* in 1956, nobody paid much attention. She did better with her next play, *The Marriage Go-Round* with old Hollywood chum Charles Boyer, but her movie swan song was the dismal *Parrish* in 1960, playing Troy Donahue's mother. Maintaining her ties with the international set, she moved to Barbados and created a showcase home at Belle Rive, a 200-year-old estate. When her second husband, Dr. Joel Pressman died, Claudette used stage acting as therapy of sorts—she didn't need the money. On tour and on Broadway, her choices proved less than box office, but everybody marveled at her ageless style. Co-starring with Rex Harrison in *The Kingfisher*, she finally had a hit, and from the late 1970s on she has rarely been out of the public eye, whether hosting the Reagans' vacation in Barbados or being honored by Lincoln Center as "one of Hollywood's most popular and durable stars, who has given us such consistent pleasure."

Our photo session is a lesson in professionalism and over in just five minutes. Claudette sweeps up her dress. "At my age the best thing is to keep going—I shouldn't do this or do that, I shouldn't be off to London and Paris and Rome and Egypt, but I *am*," she says. "You know that story about Alfred Lunt on the eve of his 80th birthday. He was complaining terribly. He was blind in one eye, had only one kidney left, and Lynn (Fontanne) said, 'Well, Alfred, at your age you'll just have to put up with life's little inconveniences.' " Her friend Doug Whitney sees us to the door. "Au revoir," calls Claudette. Then *sotto voce* Whitney lets us in on a little secret. "Claudette's been ill but didn't want to disappoint you. She got out of her sickbed to do this. You should see her on a good day."

BEULAH BONDI

To the very end, it was a full life. When Beulah Bondi died in 1981, the result of a freak accident—she fell trying not to step on her beloved Mr. Cat—she was four months short of her 93rd birthday, and proud of every year. "Oh, they won't let me drive anymore," she would complain, but that did not stop her gallivanting. She had just returned from Washington State the afternoon we met her and was directing the trimming of some eucalyptus trees. They had encroached on her second-floor terrace, from which Beulah could look down on the Hollywood that had given her a unique career. The Spanish-style house with a quaint turret was once home for James Hilton, and later Rosalind Russell, but for 40 years Beulah, a good businesswoman, had lived there and filled it with her travel treasures. She had circled the world twice and at 90 gone by steamer to Australia. Two columns from a Spanish church, circa 1460, divided the living room from the dining area, and a menagerie of small animals, mostly elephants, and other collectibles were everywhere. The only giveaway that an actress resided here was the fan mail on the hallway desk.

In 1963 Beulah voluntarily retired for eight years. She started up again with a handful of impressive television guest roles in the 1970s. But the mail never ceased. And Beulah loved that. She was soft-spoken, realistic. She knew her work was good and always smiled slyly when told she was the greatest character actress of Hollywood's glory days. She would add, "But I'm a good cook, too, you know." Beulah never longed for the star part. "I found my pleasure early, I guess when I was seven or so, I just knew I wanted to act," she explained. "I had sense enough to realize I was no beauty." She made her stage debut in 1901 with a stock company. She toured in regional companies "until I was really ready" and didn't hit Broadway until she was 37. She created a sensation as the

nosy gossip in Elmer Rice's *Street Scene,* and King Vidor insisted she repeat the role in his 1931 film. During the next 32 years, Beulah made 64 movies for the finest directors—John Ford, William Wyler, Cecil B. DeMille, Leo McCarey and Frank Capra. She supported the biggest names and played James Stewart's mother five times—and again in his 1971 television series. Beulah would never name her favorite roles. But Granny Tucker, the old crone who wouldn't come in from the rain in Jean Renoir's *The Southerner,* and her single starring role in McCarey's *Make Way for Tomorrow,* in which she and Victor Moore played rejected parents who had to separate because their children would not take them in, were very dear to her. Both flopped, but she witnessed their rediscovery. Beulah could kick up her heels, too, and many fans relish the scene in *Vivacious Lady* when she partnered Charles Coburn, Ginger Rogers and James Ellison to do the Big Apple. She had two major disappointments—not winning an Oscar though twice nominated (*The Glorious Hussy, Of Human Hearts*) and losing the part of Ma Joad in *The Grapes of Wrath.* John Ford cast her and she even prepared for it by visiting migrant camps, only to have 20th Century-Fox boss Darryl F. Zanuck replace her with his contract player Jane Darwell.

Yet Beulah maintained she was "the luckiest actress in the world . . . I worked with the best, I gave my best." When she won an Emmy for her 1976 appearance in *The Waltons,* she was genuinely moved "to have such an award so late in life." Ironically, Beulah never seemed to age. She played older than her years for most of her career and then was almost too youthful in her old age to seem much beyond 70. Her final appearance was on the American Film Institute television tribute to James Stewart in 1980. Henry Fonda introduced her simply: "Beulah Bondi, one of Hollywood's most beloved actresses."

ELSA LANCHESTER

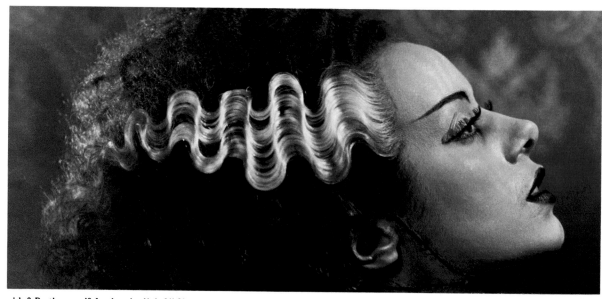

Welcome. What can I offer you—ice water or cocaine?" With the irresistible impish grin that has made Elsa Lanchester one of the whimsical wonders of the century, the widow Laughton (Charles died in 1962) is having a bit of fun with the strangers at her door. "Please say ice water! I have this new ice-making refrigerator and I'm just in love with the thing. You see, I fall in love with machines all the time. I'm Xerox-happy too (it came in handy while she was finishing her autobiography). How many of the old birds you are photographing can tell you how much they love their Xerox machine?" The conversation is going to be one-sided. "Out-

side? By the pool? In the *daylight?*" She screams the words. "I'm old! Be kind! Not the sunlight!" Elsa was born in the Lewisham district of London in 1902, "a magnificent bastard, you of course know all about that." She paddles through the small kitchen, stopping in front of the new refrigerator to do a little jig of joy. In the walled garden by a rundown pool, she starts playing with a hanging cactus. "It's donkey's tail, but Charles always called it donkey's dong." She pronounces the setting all wrong. "Inside, inside, I say. March, everybody march." As we troop back through the kitchen, Elsa does a reprise in front of the ice-maker.

Settling in front of a 1957 painting by Tadashi Sato, she slyly waves and says, "Boo!" in honor of *The Bride of Frankenstein,* her most memorable movie. "I'll put Vaseline on my cheeks if you think I'm not bright enough as myself, Mr. Horst." Elsa then rattles on about art. "The paintings, well, it was either a house without art or my being out on the street with the art." The bulk of the collection she and Laughton put together has been disposed of, but there remains a Morris Graves, a Nicholas de Stael and a beautiful Jean Le Moal, and some good

samples of Southwest Indian crafts. She points to one painting. "That's me. I'm 12 in that. Know how I can tell? My bust."

In the prologue of *The Bride of Frankenstein,* playing Mary Shelley, Elsa has the line: "Audiences need more than a simple little love story." The words were prophetic. In her autobiography, she tells the poignant story of two rare artists who lived and worked together for 33 years, yet led separate lives. "It was hard to write so personally, but I've done my best." In her book she talks about Laughton's homosexuality. Learning he has had sex with a young man "on our sofa, the only thing I said was, 'Fine, okay, but get rid of the sofa.' " A boundless artist, it may have been harder than

she ever admitted to play second fiddle so often to Laughton. She always survived injustices, starting with a wild, impoverished childhood, when her suffragette mother sent her off with the Isadora Duncan dancers. By her late teens, Elsa had made a mark in the post-World War I theater scene in London, and in a long career she moved up from gamin to diseuse to classical character actress, playing everything from a great Ariel at the Old Vic to the monster's electrified mate to cabarets to Disney eccentrics.

In the fall of 1983, Elsa's blithe spirit was struck down by a stroke. True to her generous nature, she worried more about the friends who were caring for her. As this roisterous charmer told us, "I guess everyone has to grow old in their own way, but I hope I keep a sense of humor until the end."

ELEANOR BOARDMAN

Of all the matchless beauties who graced the movies, Eleanor Boardman is the connoisseur's dream. Her aristocratic bearing and fine-boned countenance were tempered by a warm serenity, something akin to the storybook romanticism we attach to royalty. She possessed those qualities in the 1920s as an MGM star and she possesses them today as a reed-thin grande dame in Montecito, the fashionable suburb of Santa Barbara. It's not unusual to find Eleanor traipsing down a runway in a charity fashion parade. "Oh, I modeled for a friend on my 80th birthday, that's what all the talk was about. But I never cared for anything that came from celebrity. The best part of my life was when I left Hollywood and lived in Europe for 12 years." Now in her ninth decade (born in Philadelphia in 1898), Eleanor is majestic. In the home she has decorated ("I moved here in 1968, I'd had too many big houses and castles in my life"), wearing a sweater she designed ("I'm a good seamstress and Marion [Davies] and I both loved to sew"), she has the regal air of a deposed duchess.

Eleanor first gained attention as the Eastman Kodak Girl after World War I. Hollywood beckoned, and in 1923, playing a minister's daughter named Remember Steddon in Rupert Hughes's *Souls for Sale*, Eleanor established herself. Yet her most glittering role was in the social circle of Hearst and Davies, Thalberg and Shearer. When she married director King Vidor (his ex-wife Florence Vidor then married Jascha Heifetz), the wedding was to be a double ceremony with Garbo and John Gilbert—but Garbo never showed. "Do you think this picture is worth anything?" Eleanor has pulled out an oversize original of her wedding party, with Hollywood's Who's Who in attendance. "If it's worth something, I'm going to sell it. You know I don't have much time left,

and I'd like to put my house in order. I always say it is easy to build a house but not a garden, and I prefer living flowers to cold walls." When the Vidor marriage failed, off she went to Europe with a new husband, another director, the temperamental Harry d'Abbadie d'Arrast, who was already washed up in Hollywood. World events caught up with them everywhere they traveled. First the civil war in Spain: "We came down that last mountain road to the border patrol with our hands locked over our heads to show that we were unarmed," she recalls, as they journeyed to his family estate, Echaux at Etienne de Baigorry, in the Basses-Pyrenees. "Then I got away nine months after the Germans came."

Divorced from d'Arrast, she settled in Beverly Hills in the gate house on friend Marion Davies's estate. Though neighbor Virginia Cherrill looks in on her now, Eleanor has no contact with the film world. Ironically, for a star born to play princesses, she is honored for Vidor's *The Crowd.* This downbeat domestic drama, made in 1928, has been hailed as "a landmark film—an apogee of silent technique." The acting of James Murray and Eleanor as the young couple facing big city despair and the death of their child continues to move modern audiences. Critics today echo what Gilbert Seldes wrote years ago: "The great player is, however, not the lead [Murray] but Eleanor Boardman . . . everything in her creation is personal, worked out from within, and terribly affecting. She brought me close to tears more than once . . . it is altogether a beautiful performance." Eleanor sighs like a queen: "Yes, *The Crowd, The Crowd,* it haunts me in the best ways, and I suppose when I pop off, I'll be kind of happy it is what's left behind."

MARY BRIAN

The Christmas movie of 1924 was a much touted film version of Sir James Barrie's *Peter Pan*, with fresh faces endorsed by the playwright himself. The film didn't live up to the buildup, but the cast did. Betty Bronson as Peter so enchanted that she was called another Mary Pickford. But the real comer turned out to be the sweetie pie who played Wendy, a Texas teenager named Louise Byrdie Dantzler. Renamed Mary Brian, she spent the next dozen years as a Paramount contractee, ingenueing her way through more than 50 popular films. Mary was in the first versions of *Beau Geste* with Ronald Colman and *The Front Page*, where, caught in the verbal barrage between Pat O'Brien and Adolphe Menjou, any youngster would grow up fast. In the third version of *The Virginian*, Mary cast a tiny shadow next to Gary Cooper's long one. She was most comfortable being romanced by her own kind, juveniles such as Buddy Rogers and Lanny Ross. In W. C. Fields's *The Man on the Flying Trapeze*, "The Sweetest Girl in the Movies" image was a fine foil for Fields's sour wit. No matter what the part, Mary retained a touch of Wendy. Any Hollywood veteran will tell you that the woman was every bit as sweet-natured as the characters she played.

The good girl tag couldn't last forever, and by the mid-1930s Mary went packing to England to try to buoy up a slumping career and turn her back on the man she loved, actor-singer Dick Powell, who had married Joan Blondell. Mary didn't marry until 1941 (*Cosmopolitan* illustrator Jon Whitcomb), and it lasted three months. In 1947 she tried again, and spent 20 years with George Tomasini, Hitchcock's personal film editor (*North by Northwest, Psycho*). Except for a season on television in 1953 playing the mother on *Meet Corliss Archer*, Mary has spent her time on her second and lucrative career, portrait painting. She bubbles in the same small ingenue voice, "You fool, anyone can act or learn to fake it, but to paint . . ." In her 70s, she's as animated as she was listening to Buddy Rogers strum a ukulele. Her North Hollywood home is on a secluded acre just a few blocks from freeway

traffic. "We used to have sheep here to keep the lawn down." In the den, the walls are filled with WWII photos and plaques of Mary's work, when she entertained troops in Europe and North Africa. "We traveled with a combat unit on the front lines. We couldn't use scenery or anything because we had to be undercover." Mary takes a chair next to one of her paintings, a favorite, of her godchild, the daughter of Stuart Erwin, Jr. Stu Sr. and his wife, June Collyer, were friends and colleagues at Paramount. "If you witness three generations in Hollywood, does that make you a pioneer? I was so young when I started, I had to go to school on the lot." Then, sounding a sensible note worthy of Wendy, she adds, "But I'm glad I've got my painting and not just my memories like so many other old-timers."

LAURA LA PLANTE

The name alone conjures up the silent screen, which gave us exotic creatures like Lya De Putti and Nita Naldi. But there was nothing exotic about Laura La Plante except the name. She was petite, pert and pretty (and still is) and such an enchanting comedienne that in the late 1920s she reigned as the queen of the Universal lot (Lon Chaney was king). Laura came from mighty hearty stock. Her mother, one of 19 children reared on a Missouri farm, worked her way through Columbia University in an age when few women got to college. Laura's father was a French dance instructor. She was born in 1904 in St. Louis, but her mother left with Laura and her sister to seek a better life in California. That life was found because dimpled, fun-loving Laura was made for movie comedy. She served her apprenticeship in Christie Comedies for $5 a day. At 19 she was one of the Wampas Baby Stars, and when Gladys Walton became pregnant, Universal elevated Laura to stardom in *Excitement*, about a thrill-seeking bride who got what she was looking for. It was Laura's 39th film. She went on to make another 40 or so, including a comeback in 1957 as Betty Hutton's mother in a drab potboiler called *Spring Reunion*. But at her zenith, Laura was a much loved stylesetter with her shingled hairdo—it never changed but did stand on end once in her best remembered movie, *The Cat and the Canary*. Laura also made a happy transition to talkies, starring as Magnolia in the first film version of *Show Boat*. If a second marriage hadn't kept her in England, she might have had a longer career. On the other hand, then as now Laura is the most modest of the great stars, laughingly admitting, "I can't sit through those old movies of mine, and I just don't understand how anybody else can." She is a friend and neighbor of Billie Dove's in Rancho Mirage. Several years ago Laura suffered a voice loss caused by spastic dysphonia. Fortunately, an operation returned her speech, but Laura much prefers to remain silent about her little appreciated career.

RUBY KEELER

Newport Beach, California. The fall of 1980. Kathy Lowe is patting the hand of her mother, Ruby Keeler, who is propped up in a chair. A nurse-therapist is standing near. "She was in a car with my sister and her husband in the middle of Montana four years ago," Kathy says with a break in her voice. "Then something awful happened. My mother said, 'Oh, I have a terrible headache,' and a second later, 'You better get me to a hospital, something is running down the back of my head, running down my neck.' It was two months before my mother said another word. She was comatose all that time, and one doctor said the aneurysm in an artery in the brain was so bad that if she *ever* pulled out, she'd never walk again."

New York City. The fall of 1981. A gala at Lincoln Center. After a dozen stars have done their acts, Ruby Keeler steps on stage and sings "I Want to Be Happy" and then goes into her dance, only a few basic steps with chorus boys but it brings the evening to a moving finale. Determined, courageous in fact, she had won the battle and added another chapter to the saga of an old hoofer who wouldn't stay down. Honesty, combined with her Catholic faith, is Ruby's strongest ally. She never doubted she would recover and she never lost hope. She speaks publicly about her illness, telling others, "Never give up. That's the worst."

As for her career, she smiles with her big puppy eyes and refuses to make any claims about her acting or singing or the way she looks up there on the screen in nine of the gaudiest, bawdiest Warner Bros. musicals ever conceived. Their popularity has made Ruby a household name for three generations as the quintessential 1930s camp chorine. Ruby admits that her dancing, a kind of head-down, clodhopper tap, isn't much good. Yet at the heart of mad dance director Busby Berkeley's outrageous spectacles ("42nd Street," "By a Waterfall," "Shanghai Lil," "The Shadow Waltz"), there is Ruby, giving it all the good college try, totally irresistible. "Well, look who was in those movies, look at the talents," she says. Indeed, with Dick Powell, Joan Blondell, Ginger Rogers, James Cagney, some of the best character actors who ever

wisecracked, plus the enduring songs of Al Dubin and Harry Warren, Ruby is part of the cultural time capsule of the Depression.

Born in Halifax in 1909, Ruby grew up in an Irish-Dutch family of five girls and a boy. When she was three they moved to the tenements of Manhattan, where her father drove an ice truck. Like many poor kids, she lied about her age and by 16 was dancing in a speakeasy where Texas ("Hello, Suckers") Guinan held forth. "She took a liking to me, but with all the gangsters around my mother still came and took me home at night." Ruby remembers Guinan's advice: "Never point at anything except the French pastry." Moving up to specialties in Broadway shows, she caught the eye of Asa Yoelson, who as Al Jolson was one of the greatest celebrities of the Prohibition era. He liked showgirls and married two before making 19-year-old Ruby his third wife. The legend is true that when Ruby danced to "Liza" in George Gershwin's 1929 *Show Girl*, Jolson would make a surprise appearance in the audience and belt the hit tune to his new bride. Four weeks after it opened, Ruby left the musical and dropped out of public view. Three years later Darryl F. Zanuck cast her as the ingenue in *42nd Street*. When the star in the plot, Bebe Daniels, breaks her ankle, the understudy, played by Ruby, is told: "You're going out on that stage a youngster but you're coming back—a *star*." Life imitated art. Ruby's fame was cemented but her marriage wasn't. Jolson was a mean egomaniac and a ladies' man. Ruby is mum on their 11 years together, allowing only, "It was a mistake, a long mistake." In 1941 she found happiness with real estate tycoon John Lowe and abandoned what was left of a burned-out career. The Lowes had three daughters and a son, and Ruby won custody of the son she adopted with Jolson.

In 1971, a widow with a grown family, Ruby made news again. Producer Harry Rigby talked her into a revival of *No, No, Nanette*. The years had been gentle to Ruby and to her talent too. For two Broadway seasons, audiences sang along when she broke into "I Want to Be Happy." Of course she had no way of knowing her bravest performance was still to come, the struggle to conquer the damage of a stroke. Rigby, who rewarded Ruby with a history-making comeback, calls her "Divinity."

FAY WRAY

When Fay Wray, the greatest screamer in movie history, heard that she was the lucky ingenue that Colonel Merian C. Cooper wanted to cast opposite "the tallest, darkest leading man in Hollywood," she naturally conjured up romantic visions of Clark Gable or Gary Cooper. "My heart raced along, waiting for the revelation," she remembers. "Then my heart sank, when Cooper held up some sketches. An absolutely enormous gorilla was staring at me." Donning a blonde wig ("well, they didn't want a brunette opposite a brunette") and holding her own with a 19-inch toy model brought to life with stop-motion photography and miniature projection, Fay was destined for immortality as Ann Darrow in *King Kong,* the moving, mythic retelling of Beauty and the Beast. "Oh, it's a major statement, all right," she says today about the 1933 classic, which has been hailed as the most moral of our sci-fi films as well as the most perverse love story ever told. "And the damned thing is around me all the time. *King Kong* just has a life of its own, and if I ever got tired of it, then I'd be tired all the time. But what a creation of imagination and exuberance!"

Fay's pre-*Kong* career was pretty imaginative too. For two of the most difficult directors she gave outstanding performances—as the virginal, crippled harpist in Erich von Stroheim's *The Wedding March* and as the double-crossing Ritzy in Josef von Sternberg's gangster melodrama *Thunderbolt.* But post-*Kong* was mostly second leads. Her first marriage, to writer John Monk Saunders, ended in divorce, and shortly thereafter he committed suicide. Her second, to screenwriter Robert Riskin, who scripted many of the Frank Capra fables (*It Happened One Night, Lost Horizon*), was happier and she retired in the 1940s to rear three children. Widowed in 1955, Fay has worked on and off ever since. Now married to neurosurgeon Sandy Rothenberg, she and her husband live in a smallish apartment in Century City, a high-rise that Kong would appreciate. Their 19th-floor flat boasts a first-rate art collection, including five Mirós, a Chagall and a Picasso (Paloma in boots). In one corner is a typed manuscript still in the works. "I'm calling my book 'Reprieve,' but it's not just about me and my career—that's not interesting. I'm not important, but the times I've passed through were truly remarkable," says the actress who began life in 1907, the daughter of a Canadian rancher. "My philosophy is simple. I look at the good values in life and I try to appreciate them." Several years ago this veteran of over 100 movies was asked to pose with one of the Kong models. Holding it on her lap, Fay couldn't resist: "It's really quite nice to have the upper hand with Kong after all these years."

129

BILLIE DOVE

I n 1928, if you queried the man on the street to name the most beautiful girl in the world, chances are the answer would come back: "The Dove." Artist James Montgomery Flagg, producer Flo Ziegfeld and eventually Howard Hughes all were held spellbound by Billie Dove, "The All-American Beauty," as her publicity handouts read when she was a First National star in the 1920s. Born Lillian Bohney in New York around 1901 ("My husbands never knew my age"), she was modeling for Howard Chandler Christy by the time she was 15. When Ziegfeld wanted her for his Follies, she declined at first, not wishing to be just another chorus cutie. But on June 12, 1917, The Follies of 1917 opened, and there, seated on a suspended hoop with a pink spot highlighting her enormous hazel eyes, was the delicáte Dove, anything but another chorus girl. The teenager did movie bits in New Jersey, and in 1923 she married director Irvin V. Willat. Not surprisingly, she was soon threatening Corinne Griffith, The Orchid Lady, as the great beauty at First National. Then Hughes entered Billie's life. He paid Willat $325,000 to divorce her, bought up her movie contract and starred her in a couple of flops, though in those early talkies Billie's voice proved a seductive complement to her looks. Hughes, alas, never offered marriage—some say that by 1933 he was taken with a Hollywood newcomer named Katharine Hepburn. Billie found solace with a second husband—naturally, another millionaire. After 37 years, that marriage failed and Billie took a much younger man for a disastrous third marriage. Today she lives and paints at her desert estate in Rancho Mirage. So potent was her exquisite spell that there's still a Billie Dove fan club, and rarely a day passes when she doesn't receive some worshipful mail, more than 50 years after her last movie, *Blondie of the Follies.*

VIVIENNE SEGAL

Vivacious, tart-tongued, too, and properly aglow as any firebrand of Broadway legend should be, Vivienne Segal in person doesn't disappoint. Larry Hart, the wittiest of lyricists, swore: "I would rather be caught dead wearing a suit I wouldn't be caught dead wearing than weather one of Viv Segal's storms." In her comfortable little house on the Beverly Hills–Hollywood borderline, Vivienne lives in relative obscurity. "Why not?" she asks. "I don't want to die with *my* boots on. I can't sing anymore, the pipes have dried up." For years she has suffered with a heart condition—"I even get a little angina making up the bed, who wouldn't, spending the end of your life making up the bed?" The face is smooth, her hands like a child's and her figure damned good. "But I'm hard of hearing," she shouts. "And I've lost my smile," she adds, referring to her cosmetic surgery."I have no nose left and I had a cartilage implant over my lip, so there goes the smile. Well, that's what you get when you monkey around with God!"

The Segal career began in 1915 when her mother pushed Vivienne into an audition for *The Blue Paradise.* In the next decade she rapidly rose to become one of those ingenue-type prima donnas so popular on Broadway in the 1920s. Her biggest hit was Flo Ziegfeld's 1928 production of Rudolf Friml's *The Three Musketeers* (she played Constance). With the coming of sound Hollywood whistled, but the tunes were for the lousiest "All-Talking, All-Singing, All-Dancing" musicals (*Song of the West, Bride of the Regiment, Golden Dawn*). The last is a camp classic. It was recently revived in London at the British Film Institute—"A rarity not to be missed." Vivienne played Dawn. Some sample songs: "Africa Smiles No More," "In a Jungle Bungalow" and "Me and My Bwanna." There would have been no Segal mystique today if her early work had petered out in the mid-1930s, which indeed it threatened to do. To the rescue came Rodgers and Hart in 1938 with the role of Countess Peggy Palaffi in *I Married an Angel.* She got to sing the plaintive "Spring Is Here (why doesn't my heart go dancing)." Changing her image, she kicked up her heels for the first time as a comedienne. Vivienne was hilarious when she and Audrey Christie impersonated all 36 girls of a chorus line in the number "At the Roxy Music Hall." Facing middle age, Vivienne came through sexy and sassy and sensational. Hart admitted she was his favorite singer; he even confessed he had fallen in love with her, though he had never shown any interest whatsoever in other women. She inspired some of Hart's most worldy-wise lyrics, material both beautiful and bitchy—and just right for Vivienne's personality. In *Pal Joey,* which opened on Broadway in December 1940, and again in its even more successful revival 11 years later, Vivienne was as sophisticated a musical stylist as the Broadway theater had ever witnessed. Playing the slumming society dame Vera Simpson, she sang "Bewitched, Bothered and Bewildered" and "Take Him (I won't put a price on him)" with devastating efficacy. Hart wrote his very last song for her in the 1943 revival of *A Connecticut Yankee*—another classic, "To Keep My Love Alive," sung by Vivienne as the wickedly amusing Morgan le Fay:

"I married many men /A ton of them /And yet I was untrue to none of them /

    Because I bumped off ev'ry one of them /To keep my love alive."

After she finished off Sir Paul, Sir Thomas, Sir Francis, Sir Athelstane, Sir Ethelbert, Sir Marmaduke, et al, to keep her love alive, audiences would go wild. Find anyone who witnessed a Segal performance and they will tell you she was unique and utterly unforgettable. Today she doesn't mind not being remembered in the same class as Gertrude Lawrence and Mary Martin. Recordings leave a vivid if limited example of her style, her vocalism. Living alone—she had two failed marriages and no children, Vivienne is without illusions. "I'm over 80 (she was born in Philadelphia in 1897), and why should I set my head out the front door. People who don't think I'm dead just want to see how old I look!"

DOROTHY McGUIRE

Before a performance of the 1976 Broadway revival of Tennessee Williams's *The Night of the Iguana,* a woman in the audience started yelling for Dorothy McGuire. The shouting got worse, then Dorothy appeared and quieted the crazed soul, leading her out of the theater. Dorothy displayed the kind of gentle strengths she brought to her memorable mother roles in *A Tree Grows in Brooklyn* and *Friendly Persuasion.* When we arrived at her Beverly Hills showcase home, once owned by silent star Corinne Griffith, Dorothy was nervous, more like the child-woman she essayed in her stage success *Claudia,* the film of which launched her movie stardom in 1943. Horst asked her to stand with her legs slightly apart. "It's not characteristic," she snapped. "And no close-ups, please no close-ups," she begged, striking a pose in front of a blowup of one of her late husband's photographs. In 1943, at the age of 25, she married photographer John Swope, heir to the General Electric fortune. His photo of their three-hour-old daughter made the cover of *Life* in 1949. Dorothy's assignments soon became more matronly and less frequent. With our photos taken, Dorothy simmered down, but she was still far from the touching mute in *The Spiral Staircase,* her finest performance.

MARTHA SCOTT

"I had an aunt who always told me that middle age doesn't start until you're 76," says Martha Scott, fingering her pearls. In that case, Martha, who was born in Missouri in 1914, has a few years left in her *youth*. Age has always played havoc with her casting. Martha's reputation rests with her Emily Webb in the historic 1938 production of Thornton Wilder's *Our Town*. She repeated the part in her movie debut, but was too old on camera for the youth of the character. At the other extreme, she aged beautifully as the small town teacher in *Three Cheers for Miss Bishop* and as the minister's wife in *One Foot in Heaven*. Downright confounding are her encounters with Charlton Heston. On stage in *Design for a Stained Glass Window* and *The Tumbler*, Martha played his wife. The same years on screen, in *The Ten Commandments* and *Ben-Hur*, she was his mother! The mother roles won out and carried her into television sitcom. "The message is that I work, and often." She also has been active as a theatrical and film producer (*First Monday in October*). With a second marriage of nearly 40 years and three grown children, Martha can look back happily. "Let's just tell people that I don't believe in age, any age, no matter how comforting what my aunt used to say."

KATHARINE HEPBURN

I'm not afraid, I'm not afraid . . . of being just a morning glory."—Katharine Hepburn as Eva Lovelace, her first Oscar-winning role, in her third movie, *Morning Glory*

Kate the fearless is sitting in the parlor of her well-worn Turtle Bay town house in mid-Manhattan. The place needs a paint job and the ceiling is beginning to peel. The aroma of home-made sausages drifts up the stairs from the kitchen, where Phyllis Wilbourn, Kate's longtime companion (whom she inherited from actress Constance Collier), is preparing dinner. "So I did things that may have seemed wildly eccentric," Kate croaks in that quivery Yankee schoolmarm voice. "But to me they only seemed sensible. I've done things that interested me and, well, a few things I did just to be sweet." Every tree she climbs—literally, every sail she sets, every damned thing Kate tackles flies in the face of convention and age. The failure rate for actresses is disgracefully high. But Kate, a fighter now as always, keeps up her guard. Peers Claudette Colbert and Barbara Stanwyck ("How I would love to have done *On Golden Pond* with Hank") speak of Hep-

burn with envy, marveling that she is still bankable.

What's the secret of this freckle-faced, angular stick who is terribly mannered and has never been particularly sexy? The answer, of course, is that she knew what she wanted and still knows how to get it. Kate has become a tough old boot, but her renegade personality has survived by force of character. Limited as an actress, she was lucky in that even when she struck out she never had to worry about the poorhouse. "Yes, I had more of a silver spoon in my mouth than a lot of people. I mean, I wasn't rich, but my father was a successful surgeon (her mother an early advocate of planned parenthood). When I made money early on, Dad saved it. He thought I wouldn't last more than five years." By being cagey with her so-called outspokenness and her tastes (Michael Jackson is a friend), her appeal cuts across any age gap. She has hidden her vanity well. "I never wear makeup and long ago I learned the joys of patched dungarees." Still, she has knocked off a few years from her birth date (1907 is the right year) and she has had a face-lift. Accidents and illnesses little faze her indomitable nature—her shakes have been visible for 20 years, and an eye infection she got from falling in the Grand Canal in Venice for a scene in *Summertime* makes her teary like a cocker spaniel. Love affairs, or rumors of them, with Howard Hughes, producer Leland Hayward and particularly Spencer Tracy may have been disappointments, as surely was the failed attempt to launch a career for her niece, Katharine Houghton, in *Guess Who's Coming to Dinner*. Kate's loyalty, though, is inviolate; she played Florence Nightingale to

sick and dying friends, first Ethel Barrymore and then Tracy. Yet when Garson Kanin wrote a book about her and Tracy, she tossed her old pal and his wife, Ruth Gordon, out of her life forever. "We can all tell things about each other," she explains, "but I think you should just shut up about friends."

Her standards are unwavering—she has never stooped to the junk that blighted Bette Davis's late career. "I think I've been the luckiest person alive because I was born at the right time *for me*. I just don't believe in retiring." The

dinner guests are arriving. "We eat early here. I live with the light," she says, heading down the stairs. Running her fingers through her pile of ruffled golden red and gray hair, she adds: "I don't think any of us are all that independent, not really independent of life and its obligations. People think, well, she's done what she wants to do when she wants to do it. Like hell I have."

JOAN BENNETT

For an actress who always said that being a mother was her favorite role (four daughters, a dozen grandchildren), Joan Bennett nonetheless was caught up in the world of powder and paint from the very beginning. Her father was the larger-than-life matinee idol Richard Bennett; her mother, Adrienne Morrison, traced her own theatrical roots back to 18th century England. Joan's oldest sister, Constance, was one of the genuine glamour pusses of the 1930s. At four Joan made her stage debut with her dad in *Damaged Goods,* a shocker about syphilis. By 16 she was a bride and by 18 a mother and divorced. Since her father was stingy and her ex-husband a drinker, Joan turned to the talkies for a living. Blonde and doll-like, she learned the trade opposite Ronald Colman, John Barrymore and George Arliss. Her best early role

was Amy in George Cukor's 1933 *Little Women.* In 1939 Joan turned brunette and deadly, entering her femme fatale stage. Forming a production company with the great German director Fritz Lang, she made two lurid film noirs, *The Woman in the Window* and *Scarlet Street,* driving Edward G. Robinson crazy with lust in both. Her taste in prestigious directors like Lang, Max Ophuls and Jean Renoir did little to make Bennett box office. After more than 60 films, she ended up playing mothers in *Father of the Bride* and *Father's Little Dividend*—her dark, middle-age looks a perfect match for "daughter" Elizabeth Taylor.

By this time Joan had divorced second husband Gene Markey (he had a thing for actresses and later married Hedy Lamarr and Myrna Loy) and settled down with producer Walter Wanger, who had her under personal contract. In 1949 at age 39, Joan toppled Marlene Dietrich as Hollywood's youngest grandmother. Dietrich cabled: "Thanks for taking the heat off." Two years later scandal struck. A jealous Wanger stalked his wife and her agent, Jennings Lang, into a parking lot and shot Lang in the testicles. Wanger went to jail for 101 days and Joan, now a grandmother with a tarnished image, saw the career sink. Still married to Wanger, she had affairs with actors Donald Cook and John Emery, Tallulah Bankhead's ex, both to end sadly with their deaths. In the late 1960s Joan recaptured some lost fame with a long stint on the ghoulish soap opera *Dark Shadows.*

In the living room of her small Scarsdale, New York, home with fourth husband David Wilde, an ex-publisher, Joan is a study in slow motion. Painfully thin, she cannot see much without thick glasses. "I was always blind, and I suffered, too, because in my day girls weren't supposed to be seen in glasses," she says in a sexy whisper. "I don't know how I got through a lot of things in my life, but I did. I always said I learned by osmosis. Well, I had to with that family of mine. And I've worked so damned many years, I don't care if it's over." In her 1970 autobiography, *The Bennett Playbill,* she summed up the "priceless privilege of having been born into the theatre. . . . The profession has given me more than my share of success, failure, love, laughter and despair. I've not a single regret for any of it."

HEATHER ANGEL

Bombed out in Bristol, torpedoed by a German sub on a voyage to show her husband their baby, who is, alas, dead in her arms, the shell-shocked Mrs. Higgins in *Lifeboat*, Alfred Hitchcock's WWII ship of fools, is a singularly pathetic creature. Trying to soften the situation, a cynical journalist acidly etched by Tallulah Bankhead offers the sad soul her fur coat. "Is it mink?" inquires Mrs. Higgins. "I hope so!" deadpans Bankhead. "Well, I always wanted one, it makes you feel kind of classy," replies Mrs. Higgins, a faint smile crossing her lips before she plunges overboard. Just as this minor Hitchcock is a microcosm of a world divided by war, the short, showy, silly role of Mrs. Higgins sums up what Hollywood did to a winsome and wistful English actress named Heather Angel. (Yes, it's her real name.) She is an accomplished, daintily pretty woman, now as then. Imported by Fox in 1932 with some fanfare as a class act, the publicity and the roles dwindled, another blatant under-use of a lovely performer. In a major production with a big-name male star, she got billed below the title. In a B programmer (she appeared in five Bulldog Drummonds), she was usually co-starred. Heather was heavenly in *Berkeley Square,* where Leslie Howard found true love in her arms by going backward in a time-lapse from 1933 to Georgian London. This film, unfortunately, has been out of circulation for years, and it's almost as difficult to turn up *Charlie Chan's Greatest Case* (it wasn't) and *Springtime for Henry,* in which Heather was her prim self but also the murderess. Making 30-plus films, she worked twice each for two masters, John Ford and Hitchcock. In the tearjerker *Pilgrimage,* her American debut, and then in *The Informer,* Ford offered Heather fittingly tender roles. Hitchcock used her only in bits. Besides Mrs. Higgins, she was "the maid" serving Cary Grant and Joan Fontaine in *Suspicion.* In television Heather fared better, with five years as Miss Faversham in *Family Affair* and then a tight little character part as Harry Truman's mother-in-law in *Backstairs at the White House.*

Sitting in her book-lined living room in the Santa Barbara foothills, Heather, who was born in 1909, is reserved and quiet. The sound of bulldozers invades her private world. Michael Douglas, the actor-producer, is building up the road. If she had ever considered leaving her home of the past 25 years, it would have been after personal tragedy struck in 1971. Married 27 years to her second husband, director Robert Sinclair (his Broadway credits: the all-star cast of *The Women* and Katharine Hepburn in *The Philadelphia Story*), she saw him stabbed to death by an intruder. Heather loves the countryside and rides her horses on the mountain trails. Kicking off her shoes to climb the rocks by the pool, Heather says, "In my years in this country, I've seen so many changes. I have been quite disappointed (she was up for Melanie in *Gone with the Wind*), though I have continued to have a career. Acting was important to me and I have made it last." When she arrived in Hollywood, *Photoplay* disclosed that she was "well-educated" and a "world traveler." Her father was a lecturer in chemistry at Christ Church College at Oxford, and she attended the right schools in England and Switzerland. By 17 she was already at the Old Vic, having made her London debut playing a boy in *The Sign of the Cross.* Soon she was touring Burma, China and Egypt. Many years later it is difficult to judge if intelligence and training soften the frustrations of blighted stardom. "In all the roles I have portrayed," confesses Heather, "none seemed to give me the opportunity I had hoped for." The fact is the lady, not the roles, always had the class.

DOROTHY REVIER

The property is choice Hollywood real estate. But the house itself is of very little value—small, in need of paint, very much a remnant of the vanishing 1920s Los Angeles landscape. Inside, the humble furnishings are accented with telltale vestiges of the fame its owner once possessed— some old stills among Christian Science pamphlets and, more poignantly, a tiny faded-yellow magazine advertisement stuck in the frame of a clouded mirror. "Dorothy Revier, famous star of Columbia Pictures, says 'the very newest and smartest vogue in the movie colony is to use *one* delicate odeur through out your toiletries. Blue Waltz is simply perfect, as the fragrance always delights me.'" Today Dorothy is as forgotten as Blue Waltz—almost. On a small table is a stack of cards, illustrated with a 1979 black-and-white sketch of Dorothy at her most seductive, circa 1932—the gift of artist Bob Harman, who had the cards printed for his idol to use for the fan mail that trickles in. Another giveaway is the Rosemary (for remembrance) Award, presented to Dorothy in 1980 by film historian Tom Fulbright. The inscription says that her "unique combination of sparkling audacity, beauty and dramatic ability was enchanting." Those qualities have faded to fragility, and Dorothy seems like the ghost of Ophelia, with a distant, haunted yet aristocratic aura. In a childlike voice, she chimes, "I

do have a soft spot in my heart for the old picture business." As indeed she should. With a musician father and an aunt who was a turn-of-the-century opera singer, Dorothy was born in a trunk in 1904 and by her teens was dancing professionally in her native San Francisco. She broke into movies in 1922 and was a Wampas Baby Star in 1925. It was her patrician profile, more than any other single quality, that made Dorothy an ideal exotic type in *The Siren, The Tigress* and *Beware of Blondes.* Her strongest role came in 1929 when Douglas Fairbanks cast her as Milady de Winter in *The Iron Mask.* "We worked 14 weeks

on that one," she remembers, "and Doug was full of fun." Harry Cohn, the notorious lecher of Columbia Pictures, was not immune to Dorothy's sorcery. He held her contract so long she was dubbed "The Caviar of Poverty Row," though the films were strictly fodder. "Not another western, Harry," became Dorothy's lament. "I guess I could have

done more, but when I wanted to audition to dance with Astaire, Harry would say 'Nope.' He always wanted me to be another Eva Le Gallienne." After riding the range with Buck Jones in *The Cowboy and the Kid* in 1936, Dorothy threw in her spurs. A second marriage, to a "Philadelphian socialite," was, she says, quite happy. Holding a copy of James Montgomery Flagg's caricature of herself, drawn maybe half a century earlier, Dorothy admits, "I'd like to have the original; it must be worth a fortune now. I have one more wish, too. I'd just like to see my star put in the sidewalk on Hollywood Boulevard."

MYRNA LOY

I guess you could say my life has been an American saga. At least that's how I see the autobiography I've been working on. I told Jim (Kotsilibas-Davis, her collaborator) we could call it 'From Bed to Bed,' but I was only joking. I'm not writing that kind of book. I'm not going to deal with the men I've known and I've known enough, enough great men, too. But I still have plenty to tell. It's been good self-analysis in my old age and I've laughed and I've cried. Boy, how I've cried." Myrna Loy stops fanning herself, a catch in her voice. Aside from Lillian Gish, Myrna is our one great star who has been a working actress for seven decades. "That's a saga right there, isn't

it?" She was born Myrna Williams in 1905 in Crow Creek Valley, near Raidersburg, Montana. Her parents of Irish and Welsh descent had a small cattle ranch, and her father was already in the state legislature at the age of 21. "See, I do have a political heritage to uphold," she says, referring to her well-publicized activities as liberal Democrat, foe of Joe McCarthy and U.S. representative to UNESCO. "I was a homely kid with freckles that came out every spring and stuck on me till Christmas. When we moved to Helena, Gary Cooper lived down the block, and he told me years later he remembered my freckles and how I used to go sliding down a hill in our neighborhood." When her father died during the 1918 flu epidemic Myrna's mother packed up daughter and son and moved to Los Angeles, where at only 15 Myrna had to go to work.

What followed is probably the most extraordinary acting career in film annals. Myrna simply played everything. In over 100 movies, nothing threw her—Creoles, dancing Chinese dolls, gypsy wildcats and black-faced waitresses (in *Ham and Eggs at the Front*), as well as murderesses, perfect wives and alcoholic mothers. Two roles really made Myrna. Rouben Mamoulian let her show off her wry sexuality as the nympho countess in the Maurice Chevalier musical *Love Me Tonight* in 1932. Then two years later, for her 64th movie part, W. S. Van Dyke cast Myrna as Nora Charles opposite William Powell's Nick Charles in the first of *The Thin Man* series, the

beginning of a legendary celluloid marriage. By 1936, Myrna was named Queen of the Movies in a national poll. "I still have the crown," she reveals, "it's purple velvet and tin, and after that, Clark (Gable, her King) always called me Queenie." Sam Goldwyn gave Myrna her favorite role, the wife of the returning soldier (Fredric March) in *The Best Years of Our Lives* in 1946. The role was small, but she was top-billed in the most popular box office hit after *Gone with the Wind* until the inflationary movie market of the 1960s. It is difficult to explain to anyone who didn't experience the film during its original release just how much emotional weight a beloved actress like Myrna brought to her portrayal. She was the American dream wife and mother for a generation.

Over the last 20 years, Myrna made an occasional movie, acted on stage, though none too successfully because of her light voice, and did some television—she was quite poignant opposite Henry Fonda in *Summer Solstice* in 1981. Myrna is a movie star first and always. On the wall of her small East Side Manhattan apartment is a picture of Powell. "To my dear, dear Myrna. With fond remembrance of those days of yore when I was very young and you were even younger. My love always, Bill." She looks at the photo, touches it lightly. "He'll be hard to write about, he was such a delight. I hope I can do him justice. And if you want to know the secret of the perfect wife I played in all our movies, well, she was really a rascal, just like me."

ANNA LEE

Above Sunset Boulevard there is a little corner of Hollywood that shall forever be England. Tea is served at four with a Great Dane standing guard. "I came to this country in 1939, but every April I still get homesick for the bluebells," says Anna Lee, the quintessential English rose with her satiny complexion and graceful manners. Even a second marriage to a Texan in 1948 didn't dent her cheery British way with things. And her third marriage in 1970 to poet-novelist Robert Nathan (his seventh!) could best be described as modern day Mr. and Mrs. Chips. They share everything, including the same birth date. On January 2, 1984, she turned 70 and he hit 90.

Unlike other British imports before her (Madeleine Carroll) or after her (Deborah Kerr), Anna never reached the very top, though John Ford lovingly displayed her beauty and talent in *How Green Was My Valley* in 1941. During the war years, Anna was consumed with the war effort—General Patton dubbed her "M.B.," Morale Builder—and then she raised a family of five children. Fans of the TV soap *General Hospital* know her today as the matriarch of the Quartermaine clan and, ever gracious, Anna says, "I thought it was a comedown, after features, to do television, but I rather like it. You become a family, not unlike the old studio days." Recently Christie's auctioned a painting, *Bronze and Silver,* by Sir William Russell Flint. It went for $37,000. Anna had modeled for both of the young women figures in the canvas over 50 years ago. "I was so surprised it turned up. I just wish I could have afforded it. Sir William told me I had the most beautiful feet in London," she confides with a twinkle. In 1983, Anna received another surprise, a belated birthday gift from Buckingham Palace. Queen Elizabeth made her a Member of the British Empire.

MARSHA HUNT

Maybe Marsha Hunt really wasn't "the most famous New York model of 1935." Maybe the Paramount publicity machine was just working overtime, reaching for a hook to herald their latest arrival out of the John Roberts Powers modeling school. But one thing is certain: of all the lanky beauties who made their way west to crash the movies, Marsha proved mighty strong for the long haul. Her strengths turned out to be not her looks, with that piquant profile, but an expressive depth of feeling she brought to every role, small or big, as well as to her own personal convictions. Some models, like Jinx Falkenburg, for example, never learned to act at all; others, like Lauren Bacall, became superstars more on manufactured personality than real ability. Marsha, however, before she was even 25, demonstrated amazing versatility. She was Booth Tarkington's *Gentle Julia,* the myopic Ichabod Crane-ish sister of the Bennett clan in *Pride and Prejudice,* both young bride and then older mother in *Joe and Ethel Turp Call on the President* and, most memorably, the suicidal unwed mother in *Blossoms in the Dust,* to name four of more than 60 movie parts. By the time she was 50, Marsha had played Shakespeare (*Twelfth Night*) on national television and Shaw (*The Devil's Disciple*) on Broadway and aged so exquisitely that the dean of American drama critics, Brooks Atkinson, compared her to the legendary Lillian Gish. If fortune and fame came to others in larger measure, Hunt's rewards are a fine record of quality, consistency and truth in a career hopefully not yet over.

Always a political creature (her father was a Chicago civic leader), Marsha has had a whole second career devoted to good causes—the U.S. Committee for Refugees, the March of Dimes, Red Cross and Cerebral Palsy. For the latter she pioneered the telethon. In the 1970s both houses of Congress entered resolutions acknowledging her work with Thankful Giving, a charity she originated. Though she was suspected of being a Communist sympathizer during the McCarthy era, and both she and her second husband, producer-writer Robert Presnell, Jr., proved innocent victims who lost work during this disgraceful period, Hunt has never been less than outspoken in her beliefs. Her last good role, albeit a tiny one, was in the film version of Dalton Trumbo's antiwar novel, *Johnny Got His Gun.*

Married since 1946, she and Presnell reside in a "very well lived-in" compound in Sherman Oaks surrounded by tennis courts and rose gardens. Scattered in the den, the day of our visit, are dozens of fashion stills from four decades ago, showing a prim and poised 17-year-old modeling Hattie Carnegies. "I think these will make a good book, a unique kind of autobiography reflecting more than just the fashions and fads of the society I grew up in," she explains. "I'd like to call it 'The Way We Wore.' " Looking quite girlish now in her mid-60s, and obviously wearing very well, Marsha can only laugh when her husband joins in: "If you keep something long enough, like your wife, it becomes valuable." Sucking in her cheeks, she replies: "He's gotta be talking about the '56 Mercedes in the garage, don't you think?"

NATALIE MOORHEAD

In the "Jollywood Jottings" for December 1930, a fan magazine predicted that in the new year moviegoers could rest assured they would not see such favorites as Greta Garbo "permanent waved" or Kay Francis "in a bungalow apron" or Natalie Moorhead "out of the Mode." In those days, Moorhead, the ideal clotheshorse of the early 1930s, traveled in the best of circles. Today only a loyal few rejoice in the memory of this petite, hipless, marcelled blonde who could talk tough and dish it out to Tracy, Gable and William Powell when the talkies were young. Actually, Tracy got his from Nat, as she's affectionately known to the elite Moorhead cult, before either performer hit Hollywood. It was in a 1927 Broadway production of George M. Cohan's called *The Baby Cyclone* that Natalie's "Baby Cyclone bob" caused a bigger sensation than their acting. As was to be the destiny of her short happy career (she retired in 1940 "with maybe just a few regrets"), Moorhead's look inevitably stole the notices. Often draped in white fox, she cultivated a sexy slouch while sporting only the top designers. "I gave away my Adrians years ago," she says, casting a wide wink toward her husband. "I don't suppose I could get into them today anyway." In her tasteful home in the hills of Montecito, there are candy and nuts on every table and an exercise bike tucked away in one corner. The snarl with which she snared so many leading men has broadened into a warm and cheery smile. For over 25 years, she has been married to Juan de Garchi Torena, a gentleman every bit as elegant as his wife, whose own accomplishments include fame as a soccer champ, Spanish-language film star and two decades as a career diplomat. Natalie first married hellion Alan Crosland, the director of *The Jazz Singer,* who was killed in a car crash ("He was his own worst enemy," she allows without elaboration), and was widowed a second time by a wealthy midwesterner. She had known Juan since the 1930s and they got together again in the 1950s. Devoutly religious, they have lived and traveled all over the world, and their Hollywood years are not something they give much thought to, though a portrait of Nat in her prime is prominently placed in the living room. "Our life has been so rich in so many ways that the acting was just one part of our happiness," she explains. Because she was never tied down to a single studio, her career was erratic and often included outings at poverty row studios where she was the only class act. *The Thin Man*, the classic 1933 Nick and Nora Charles mystery, is her best work as well as choice Moorhead. As the conniving mistress-secretary to the Thin Man himself, she is a marcelled menace of the first water, at once a fashion plate and the epitome of the hardboiled dame whose type vanished from our movies and books just about the time Natalie Moorhead gave up Hollywood and went "out of the Mode."

TERESA WRIGHT

Bette Davis as Regina Giddens to Teresa Wright, playing her daughter, in the Samuel Goldwyn film version of *The Little Foxes:* "Why Alexandra, I used to think you were all sugar water."

And that's how a lot of Hollywood folks first thought of the 23-year-old ingenue Goldwyn imported from Broadway in 1941 to be his resident "girl next door." Teresa Wright fooled them. No cookie-cutter cutie, Teresa got off to a rousing start. She won Oscar nods for her first three movies. In 1942 she was nominated for best actress for *The Pride of the Yankees* as well as best supporting actress for *Mrs. Miniver,* which she won. Then, thanks to Alfred Hitchcock, who was looking for an all-American type, her fourth outing was *Shadow of a*

Doubt, Hitch's favorite among all his work. As the niece and namesake of a merry widow murderer named Charlie (played to smooth perfection by Joseph Cotten), Teresa was the essence of lost innocence in this masterpiece, which has been called the dark side of *Our Town* (Thornton Wilder worked on the screenplay). Two years later, in 1946, she was the daughter in *The Best Years of Our Lives,* and at this juncture she should have been able to write her own ticket. But today Teresa allows that she "basically hated the Hollywood game." She wouldn't do publicity, particularly pinup posing, and settled into a 10-year marriage to novelist Niven Busch, rearing two children. Her last decent parts were in *The Men,* cast opposite Marlon Brando in his film debut in 1950, and in *The Actress,* playing the mother of Jean Simmons, who was only 11 years her junior, in 1953.

Divorced, Teresa headed back to Broadway, scoring in William Inge's *The Dark at the Top of the Stairs,* followed by some impressive Emmy-nominated television roles. She was the original Annie Sullivan in the Playhouse 90 production of *The Miracle Worker* and played photographer-journalist Margaret Bourke-White in a moving biography. From her sparsely furnished West Side Manhattan apartment, she sighs when discussing her past. "You want to know the truth? When Goldwyn signed me, I didn't intend to stay. I loved the stage." During the last decade Teresa has indulged that love. Her second marriage to playwright Robert Anderson over, she works steadily. Whether playing the tragic Mary Tyrone in *Long Day's Journey into Night,* the scatterbrained mother in *You Can't Take It with You* or the wife whose husband has been carrying on for years with her sister in *Morning's at Seven,* Teresa could never be accused of being "all sugar water."

FLORENCE ELDRIDGE

I like being an age when I don't have to worry about the wrinkles," says Florence Eldridge in her 80th year. But then this most self-effacing of our preeminent actresses never indulged in vanity and as a result never received the public recognition accorded her peers. Florence was the critic's choice. And she never voiced indignation toiling in the shadow of her famous husband, Fredric March. When they met in 1926, he was a greenhorn and she had already starred on Broadway as Daisy in *The Great Gatsby* and the stepdaughter in *Six Characters in Search of an Author.* March was a consummate actor—usually he is ranked second only to Spencer Tracy as our finest dramatic screen performer. The Eldridge legacy is less defined. Florence's style wasn't showy and only on occasion did her reserve give way to florid display— in *The Greene Murder Case* she fought Jean Arthur to the finish on a roof overhanging the Hudson River (Jean lost), and her Elizabeth I took the notices from Katharine Hepburn's Mary of Scotland in John Ford's film. Florence's matronly virtues are captured best in two late 1940s movies, both co-starring March: the film version of Lillian Hellman's *Another Part of the Forest* and that sympathetic treatment of euthanasia, *An Act of Murder.*

All through the Hollywood years, during which they reared two adopted children, the Marches never really deserted the theater. "Freddy always said we were *mad* for the stage and we did take chances, all worth the taking." They also displayed a sense of humor. In 1938,

when *Yr. Obedient Husband* flopped, they ran an ad in *The New York Times* showing a cartoon of two high-wire artists missing each other. The caption exclaimed: "Oops, Sorry." Not until 1942, when they joined Tallulah Bankhead in Thornton Wilder's goofy fable about the survival of mankind, *The Skin of Our Teeth,* did the Marches enjoy a total triumph together. The play won a Pulitzer. As the earth mother, Mrs. Antro-

bus, Florence brought depth to a sketchy, one-note role that laid down an emotional base for Wilder's tomfoolery. It was to be 15 years before their next stage success as a team.

Though public-spirited (in 1943 they traveled 35,000 miles touring USO camps), the Marches, long political activists, were named as subversives in the publications *Red Channels* and *Counterattack.* The evidence had something to do with their gift of an ambulance to the Republicans in Spain's Civil War. Righteous fighters, they sued for

libel and won a complete retraction. When they starred in Arthur Miller's *An Enemy of the People* in 1950 (it closed after just 36 performances), police patrolled the theater to prevent incidents because of the reputations of both stars and playwright. In 1957 they debuted Eugene O'Neill's autobiographical play, *Long Day's Journey into Night.* Praise was boundless, March was hailed as America's greatest living actor and Florence shared the unanimous acclaim. She was heart-crushing as Mary Tyrone, the dope-crazed wife of a parsimonious old matinee idol. As her character drifted into a dreamlike retreat in the final moments, Florence made the "But I was happy for a time" soliloquy one of the memorable scenes in American theater history. Nothing could top the O'Neill achievement.

When her husband died in 1976, Florence sold the New England home, Firefly Farm, and gave up a New York City apartment. "I've moved around a lot since Freddy left me and I'd probably rather have lived back east, but my brother is out here," she explains, sitting in the living room of her Santa Barbara condo. "But I keep busy." She traveled to China with her daughter and son-in-law. She takes adult education classes. "It's T. S. Eliot I'm studying now and he isn't easy." Among Braques and Klees in the art-filled room is a small, delightful sculpture of her husband as the pirate Lafitte, from Cecil B. DeMille's *The Buccaneer.* "Hardly a typical role," she says, smiling. Neither of the Marches was typical in their careers, separate or together. For theirs was a quest for quality in everything they did.

GLORIA SWANSON

The scene was unreal. Hordes of curiosity-seekers were trying to squeeze into the gowns, sizes four and six; others were manhandling egret feathers and Lalique perfume bottles. The glory that was Gloria Swanson was up for grabs, and when the auction ended, the tattered gold-thread Salome scarf from the finale of *Sunset Boulevard* had brought $8,000. But this was not the end of the indomitable star who died in the spring of 1983. The real Swanson treasures are stored away at the University of Texas, not to be opened until the year 2000, presumably in deference to the family of Joseph P. Kennedy, Sr., who might be embarrassed by the love letters he wrote to Gloria when she was his mistress. Gloria told most of her own story—but not everything—in her autobiography, a tale brimful of sex and marriages (six), lovers and abortions.

But aside from the personal notoriety, there is no question hers was one of the important careers in film history. Her performances, too little seen today, defy age, just as she did. From Mack Sennett comedies and early DeMille (he said, "The public, not I, made Swanson a great star") to her Oscar-nominated work in *Sadie Thompson* and *The Trespasser,* Gloria was magnificent.

If in her old age she jumped off the deep end proselytizing about "the poisons in our food that are killing us," she managed to remain a beloved if eccentric public figure. She certainly never fit anyone's standard of beauty. Surprisingly small at slightly under five feet, she stood tall, maybe because her head was too big for her body, as if she had been in an elevator that fell and the pressure had pushed everything up. Her scooped-out nose rivaled Bob Hope's, and she often said her Polish, Swedish, Italian, French and German blood was a uniquely American mix. She was a fash-

ion plate for over 60 years, and it seemed that she would go on forever. Garbo once asked, "Gloria, how you wear me out. Where do you get all this energy?" Shortly before her death, Gloria said, "I don't even want a tombstone—people will remember me in their hearts or not at all." It was never ascertained exactly what her age was— 84, 86 or close to 90. Perhaps she *is* ageless, thanks to *Sunset Boulevard.* Gloria lives on as Norma Desmond, fiercely reliving the past and proud of her triumphs. Her Fifth Avenue maisonette was overflowing with honors and awards and trophies. One proclaimed: "Gloria Swanson is The Greatest Star of Them All and the Idol of Cast, Staff and Crew of *Sunset Boulevard.* June 20, 1949."

161

LORETTA
YOUNG

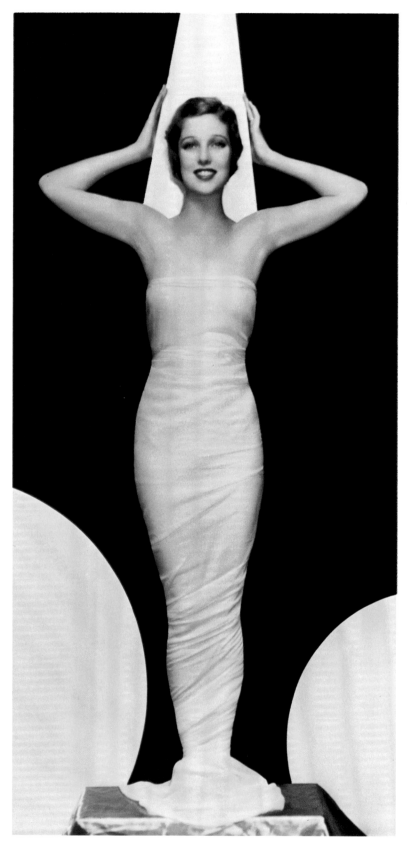

A testament to sheer force of star power, Loretta Young has miraculously survived over 20 years of voluntary retirement without a wrinkle in her glamorous fame or her flawless, face-lift-free countenance. Like such quintessential movie queens as the late Joan Crawford and Marlene Dietrich, Loretta, now in her 70s (she was born Gretchen Michaela Young in Salt Lake City in 1913), maintains an eternal screen persona—chic and ageless. Unlike many of her peers, she won't compromise the image with a quickie comeback or cameo guest bit, or by writing a confessional detailing her affairs with Clark Gable or Spencer Tracy. "Heavens, I couldn't do that—too many people might be hurt if I wrote the truth."

It is hard to believe, but Loretta made her movie debut in 1917 or 1918 as a screaming child on an operating table in a Fanny Ward tearjerker. Fanny always claimed to have discovered the fountain of youth. But if any star could make that claim, it's Loretta. "It's the genes," she says matter-of-factly, stating that her mother, the Hollywood decorator Gladys Belzer, continued to do assignments into her 90s. A proponent of positive thinking, she believes that it is never too late for self-improvement. At 67 she kicked the nicotine habit by going through six days at the Schick Clinic "and gaining the 10 pounds I always wanted." A rare negative comment concerns her home. "I have the smallest house in Beverly Hills, no room for a garden. Never buy a house when you are unhappy," she says, referring to the breakup of her second marriage. Past troubles with her children and lawsuits over her television series have left no visible scars. She is gracious to the point of embarrassment, asking Horst to help pick out the right gowns for the photographs. As Horst starts shooting, Loretta confesses she has always been self-conscious about her swan neck, an ideal for a Sargent painting. "Now I know it's an asset. Some actresses had terrible times with their necks. Connie Bennett got two terrible lines by age 45. She laughed them off, called them her Cleopatra necklace."

Once dubbed the Iron Madonna for her fierce Catholicism and tough professionalism, today Loretta prefers charity work to exploiting her classic beauty. As a volunteer at the Elisabeth Kübler Ross hospice for the terminally ill, Loretta was giving a foot massage to a patient named Ernie one day when she noticed her movie with Gary Cooper, *Along Came*

Jones, on television. She couldn't resist. "Ernie, that's me up there. How do you like it? He wiggled his toes and said, 'I think I like you better in the flesh.' Well, Ernie got an extra 10-minute rub, I can tell you."

Still, Loretta is a permanent fixture of Beverly Hills society and inevitably the most stunning woman present. To see her sweep into a room (just like the famous doorway entrances on her television show) is to witness stardom at full sail. When she is discovered in the audience of a Broadway show, all eyes have a hard time not drifting from the stage to her Nefertiti profile silhouetted in the dark. Physical beauty, though, has never sustained lasting stardom. "I learned to act by trial and error over a long period of time. Frank Capra (he directed her in *Platinum Blonde* with Jean Harlow) taught me a basic lesson: Acting is what you think. You must listen to the other actor, acting *is* what you are thinking." When Loretta listened, her doe eyes could melt an audience. Darryl F. Zanuck once ordered a scene reshot because she stood out too much. "That," she told her boss, "is exactly what I had in mind." But Loretta was also strong and smart behind the camera. "I found more pleasure from my TV series than all those movies"—because she was also her own producer, her own boss.

There should be a role or two left for Loretta, and the offers continue. "It would have to be something like a female Beckett." She pauses. "It's not important for me to see myself on the screen again, I had a great career." With the deaths of Merle Oberon and Dolores Del Rio, the retirement of Madeleine Carroll in Spain, and the reclusive Dietrich hidden away on the Avenue Montaigne in Paris, Loretta has no challengers as the last and the most beautiful star from the golden age in Hollywood.

INDEX